1240 to 3:16

How I Changed

My Legacy

By Victor Muniz

Dedication

This book is dedicated to my mother and father, who despite their craziness, gave me the right morals. Also, to my son, my pride and joy.

Epigraph

1240 to 3:16: How I Changed My Legacy is my attempt to spread the message of Godly forgiveness by reflecting on my life. As you read my story, I hope you will remember these two statements:

1. *God forgives you* regardless of what you have done
2. If you really want to change your life, *you must also forgive*

I don't know how to be more real than this.

Table of Contents

Foreword

I've been married to Victor Muniz for 19 years. The transformation that I've witnessed in these years has been nothing short of extraordinary, but that's who God is right? Extraordinary.

When we first started dating, Victor was recently released from jail, for the last time. At the time Victor was 46 years old, street tough and he'd been through a lot. He had spent 30 years of his life in an out of prison. We had many long talks. Victor was always open and honest about sharing his past with me. I was slowly learning all about him, what he had been through and what he had done. Honesty was always very important to him. Victor wanted me to know everything about him and he wanted to know everything about me, leaving us no doubt about what we were about to get into and what baggage we both could and would bring to the relationship. It was scary to me but so necessary.

I was 29 years old. I had some baggage that I brought to the relationship, but Victor's baggage was deep. Deep. Deep. I grew up in the same neighborhood, but during a different time and my upbringing was just different than his. I listened to Victor's stories and I was amazed, afraid, astonished that all of this could be a life of someone who grew up where I grew up? It's funny that we live in our own little boxes and assume that everyone is living a similar life, especially someone just like you. I was hesitant to start a relationship with him for various reasons, mostly fear, but my heart was his and I knew that I was supposed to be with this man for the rest of our lives. I stepped out in faith, and what a journey it's been.

The beginning was rough, as most marriages are. We had lived together briefly before we got married and we'd had long, long, long conversations but now this was real. We'd made a commitment and we were in. Aside from all the idiosyncrasies of learning how we each live, we continued to learn more about each other's pasts and how we were raised; our likes, our dislikes and reactions to things that happened in our daily lives. We argued. We stopped speaking. I wondered if this was going to work. He never wavered. Victor was always willing to work it out.

Victor started his walk with God early in our relationship. As soon as he came home from jail, even before we started dating, he started going to church with his father. Victor made a commitment and he kept it. He wanted to change, and he meant it. It wasn't easy. Walking with God isn't easy as we know but I'm glad I got to watch. There were times when he'd tell me in the beginning how proud he was of himself and that he couldn't believe that he'd reacted or not reacted a certain way and I'd look at him puzzled because I had seen him lose his temper over something I thought was minor. For example, we went to the Puerto Rican Day parade in June of our first year together and we were standing with our family and friends watching the parade when a group of rowdy young guys started acting out behind us. Our family and friends included small children, including my then two-year old daughter, who was in a stroller. Victor started having some words with the rowdy guys that quickly escalated to his godson and one of our other friends starting to step in. It was getting ugly, fast. I became so angry that I put my daughter into her stroller and just started walking away. Victor quickly caught up to me and tried to explain but getting the silent treatment from me, let it go for the moment. Needless to say, when Victor spoke of how proud he was of himself and how he was changing, I'd be thinking "What?!?! You were in a stupid argument about nonsense the other day." At that time, I'd heard his stories about his temper, but I still didn't get it. I didn't get that he was growing and that what I was seeing was a big change.

I watched him and am still watching him grow and change like the first time we went to Sesame Place. Victor was like a small child. He was having so much fun that he didn't want the day to end. When we went to Disney a few years later, Victor wore us out. He'd wake us up early saying, "Chop, Chop" and we'd go have breakfast, go the park until lunchtime, go back to the hotel to play in the pool and then go back to the park until it closed and start all over again the next day. Victor had a ball. He was in all the pictures with the characters. He'd never had the time to have childlike fun. As I look back on his life stories and reading this book, my heart breaks for the little boy that was never a little boy.

Even when we moved to Pennsylvania, I watched him slowly grow. He had a hard time at work. My husband is a born leader so it's easy for him to take charge and responsibility for things. He is a helper too, whether you want it or not. I tell him he's not a superhero all the time. So, what does a person who is a born leader and helper do? He became the president of the union at his job. Oh boy. He had changed but the temper was still flying. He'd go from being angry at the company over some rule infraction to being angry at the person he was representing. There was a lot of backstabbing and some painful incidents that occurred during this time, but he persevered. Victor is not a quitter because he takes his commitments seriously. There were sleepless nights and too many headaches. I told him to quit multiple times because I couldn't stand to see him this way, but he persevered. Through this I saw change. I saw him getting better at keeping his temper in check and having calmer conversations all while learning to let go when someone he helped turned on him. I saw it, but I still didn't get it. He'd tell me how much better he was doing and I'd think, "Just last night you wanted to rip that guy's head off and you're still talking about the lady you helped last month that was talking behind your back." I didn't get it. It took me years to get it.

I started getting it when I started seeing the change. When he wasn't getting into arguments about small things, when he wasn't upset about a certain behavior or certain attitudes he perceived he was

8

receiving from other people. When he wasn't assuming the worst in every situation. When he started speaking positively. When I started seeing those things change over time, it struck me that he had come even further than I knew. I really started honing in and listening to the stories of his past from a different perspective. I really started hearing him and realizing that he had come a long, long way.

When he joined the prison ministry and became the director of the ministry at our church, I was so happy for him. He'd found his place. Victor knew what his life story had led him to. He could speak to it and with his helper's heart, he could try to guide someone towards a better path than the one he had taken. I've watched God do a mighty work in my husband and I am so very proud of him and how he's sharing his life, his testimony and his desire to help others. I pray that you read this book and don't feel sorry for the little boy or stay angry at the young man in his early years making mistakes but see a little bit of yourself and how much God loves. Like the love of my life says, "If God can change me, then he can change you and if I could only help one person, then that person can help another and another and another."

Happy Reading!

Myriam

Prologue

I always knew that my journey was unique and needed to be shared with the world so it could help people. It took me over 40 years to get the courage to write this book. We all have excuses. Mine were cancer, hepatitis C, tragedy, and focus. I finally decided to pick up a pen and illustrate my journey in words at age 64. I wanted to complete the book before I turned 65 years old in September of 2018. It wasn't until I started getting involved with prison ministry and writing to inmates, that I realized how much I had procrastinated.

I thought about sharing my story as a book at least once a week, but something was missing. So, I went to the person I trusted most, my wife Myriam, and told her that I wanted (and needed) to write this book. My wife and I would get excited and start the book, but it would fizzle quickly and months would go by without any progress. I couldn't get it together. I started getting mixed feelings, worrying more about other people than myself. I didn't want to hurt anyone in this process, but I needed to be real. I had to remind myself that it was okay to be honest, so I adopted the motto, "You aren't talking about nothing but the truth." This motto helped to open a door I never knew existed, and I realized that I wasn't downgrading anyone. Instead, I was focusing on my path to forgiveness; forgiveness of myself, my family, my situations, and my faith. While it was easy for me to create many excuses, I really believe that my life and telling my story has been on God's time.

How to Navigate This Book

1240 to 3:16: How I Changed My Legacy, is divided into phases of my life's story that I have placed into three parts. **Phase 1: My Early Life** is about my life growing up in New York city as a child and the relationships I have had with the closest members of my family. In this phase you will learn about an enraged father, the love between a son and his mother, and among other things, the anger of the murder of a loved brother. **Phase 2: The Journey to 1240** is about reacting to anger, poor choices like drug addiction and street hustling, that lead to bad consequences and life lessons in prison. In Phase 2 you will discover that there are other ways to be imprisoned besides being in a cell. In **Phase 3: Changing My Legacy** you will read about how I changed my legacy by surrendering to God and how forgiveness has changed my life. This phase describes how you may change your legacy too, even when you believe there's no hope. Each phase has a series of events that narrate my life's story.

Phase 1: My Early Life (Chapters 1-12)
- Born and Raised (1-7)
- Extended Family (8-9)
- Being a Man (9-12)

Phase 2: The Journey to 1240 (Chapters 12-24)
- Drug Use (12-16)
- The Drug Game (17-18)
- Prison (20-24)

Phase 3: Changing My Legacy (Chapters 25-30)
- A Real Change (25-26)

- Fully Surrendering (27-28)
- From Struggles to Ministry (29-30)

Finally, the book wraps up with an **Epilogue: Real Talk With Victor**, where you will read about how surrendering to God helped me be free. In Real Talk, I connect my life experiences to the truth of God's perfect plan.

Epilogue: Real Talk With Victor
- For God So Loved The World
- Honor Your Father and Mother
- Do Not Take Revenge
- With God All Things Are Possible

My desire is that this book will connect with everyone who reads it. While I regularly talk to brothers in jail through the prison ministry, I want this book to reach an even wider audience. My story is not singular. Many, if not all, of us have seen someone in my shoes. I hope that I can help others avoid the mistakes I went through and that this book will spread from one person to another.

PHASE 1: MY EARLY LIFE

Living in New York City is challenging enough for a young kid, but adding an abusive and alcoholic father plus the death of my only brother made my childhood even more complicated. I lived in a state of fear, anger, and resentment. This stuck with me as I grew, which set the tone for my future. I lost myself in the chaos of my early life and couldn't see a way out.

CHAPTER 1

EARLY MEMORIES

My family included my grandparents, three uncles, and three aunts who all came from Puerto Rico. My father's name was Jorge Muniz and my mother's Maria Teresa DeJesus. I was told that my mother fell in love with my father when he was singing at night clubs in Puerto Rico. My father was 22 and my mother was about 14 years old at the time. They didn't stay in Puerto Rico long though. My mother became jealous of other women who were attracted to my father, so they moved to New York to change their lives. Part of this change was supposed to mean that my father was going to stop singing, but he didn't. Instead, he found new places to sing in New York. Most of the time my father would sing at bars, which quickly became his second home.

Our family, like many families, was dysfunctional. One of my earliest memories is of my father hitting my mother. It was a daily act. So much so that the precinct knew me when I called. It got to the point that after I told a dispatcher that I lived at 171 East 115th Street, the response would be, "Okay. We'll be there Victor." Back then, men didn't get arrested when they hit women; the police would pick them up and drive them half a mile away and tell them to cool off by walking home. At times, the police would threaten to come back and arrest the men, but they rarely did. My father would come home and give my mother the cold shoulder, not speaking to her, but he wouldn't hit her again that night. But then the next argument would escalate again, and my father would hit her again.

My older brother, Jorge Muniz, who we called Junior, was born on September 21, 1951. He was the first child and grandchild in the family, so he quickly became the favorite. When Junior was born, my parents lived on 3rd Avenue between 114th and 115th Street. At that time, we lived in a tense area. There was always fighting in the neighborhood between the Puerto Ricans and Italians, because each group was very territorial. There were no projects back then. The buildings were five or six stories with railroad apartments, fire escapes and the Super of the building usually lived in the basement. The Super took care of the building's maintenance needs. One of my mom's family members lived there as well. I am pretty sure he was my cousin. He was sick and a little crazy. Because of this and the tense fighting in the neighborhood, my mother feared for the safety of my brother. So, she sent Junior to live with my grandmother when he was less than a year old, and my grandmother refused to give him back. My mother was heartbroken and decided she wasn't going to have another child, but she happened to have me. After being separated from Junior, my mother decided that she would not let me go, and I lived with her all of my life. Well, all of her life.

I was born in Metropolitan Hospital in New York on September 8, 1953, and we quickly moved to 171 East 115th Street between 3rd and Lexington. This is the first home I actually remember. My father was offered a job as a Super which meant, at that time, we could live in the basement. As mentioned earlier, a Super is the person that takes care of the building, usually when things get broken in an apartment like a plumbing issue or heat issue.

Even though it was a basement apartment, we had a little yard. There were two bedrooms, and all the rooms were on top of one another. It was small and at the very back of the building. The only way to get to the apartment was to walk through the basement. There was a door on the right-hand side that led to a small room that my father was renting to an elderly man from the neighborhood. Once you walked past the room, there was a second door leading into the big room with the building's boiler. Then, the very next door was our apartment. I had my own bedroom, but I shared with Junior when he came over and my parents had their own bedroom. There was one bathroom and a small kitchen, which was considered a nice size during those years. We lived there for years, but it wasn't a happy life. In fact, very few things changed from the story I was told about how they met: my father still continued to sing at clubs and bars and my mother continued to love his singing. I remember my father singing this one song, "La Novena," (The Novena) to my mother regularly. When he got to the line "mi patria me lo pidio," (my country asked me) she would cry every time. The song was about a woman whose only son was drafted into the army and describes how the country asked her for her only son. I'm not sure why my mom enjoyed the song, but it seemed as though they really loved each other.

Everyone has their weaknesses, and my father's weakness was drinking. He would come home drunk and it caused my parents to argue. My mother would complain to him that he was never home and didn't contribute to the house, which always resulted in her getting hit. They had a love/hate relationship, but seeing her beaten, broke my heart. Even at 6 years old, I was angry. I wanted to help her. I remember jumping on my father's leg, giving her the chance to run away. But, I was too small to physically help her. He would shake me off, throwing me against a wall.

I was angry at my father because of how treated my mother. As a reaction, I even started trying to convince my mother to hit him while he was sleeping. One day, my father came stumbling home. He was more drunk than I had ever seen him. My father staggered to bed, toppling into it. I took the advantage of the opportunity. I had played in the abandoned building next door, and knew there was a 2X4 with a rusty nail sticking out of a corner. I quickly ran to get it and pushed it into my mother's hands. I cried, "He's sleeping. Hit him! Hit him and run." My father wasn't a big man, but my mother was only 4'10" and wasn't a fighter. She was fragile. My mother hesitated, but I was persistent. The 2X4 looked gigantic in her hands. I remember the nervous fear spread on her face, but I continued to encourage her.

My father was passed out drunk as she gathered her strength and hit him across his head with the 2X4. "Run, Mami! Run!", I blurted. Our apartment was in the basement, and I watched as she ran past the boiler to the other room. Her footsteps mixed with his screams. "Teresa! Teresa! Come. Clean me up. Put a bandage on me!" I begged her not to go. I kept telling her he would hit her again. But the yelling continued. "I'm not going to do anything to you. Come put a bandage on me," my father yelled. And she did. My mother left the safety of the other room and put some Mercurio and a Band-Aid on the long scratch over his eye. My father put his arm delicately around my mother, kissed her, and then started beating her again.

I cried, telling her that I warned her about going back. I was too scared to call the police because he was bleeding and I thought they would arrest her. Yet, in my heart, I felt a little victorious because he had a gash over one eye. It was almost like we won because my mother started to gain the courage to stand up for herself.

Not much changed after that. My father continued to visit his favorite bar, the Barcelona, between 116th and Lexington. The Barcelona regularly had parties and he would sing. One day when my mother was sick at home, my father was supposed to bring her money to buy some items from the store. When he didn't show up, my mother's demeanor changed. She became aggressive and gathered all of his clothes and put them on a dolly, one of many that rested in the basement. My father used them for his job as a Super. I followed my mother as she walked the few blocks from our house to the bar. I pushed the dolly the whole way, trailing behind her. When she found him drunk and singing, she screamed, "Jorge! Since you're here more than you are in your house with me and your son, you might as well live here. Don't come back to the house." I was in awe. On the way home, we were both scared since we didn't know when my father would be back and how he would react. That night we waited, but he didn't come home. Maybe it was because my father finally listened to his friends, but when he arrived the next day, he didn't hit her. Instead, my father hit me for the first time shortly after.

My father's drinking continued, and I became the target. This was the last straw for my mother. My mother was in the shower and I was jumping on the bed. I lit a match and set fire to the four corners of the mattress. I honestly don't know if there is a reason why this came into my mind, it just felt like something to do. I thought I was having fun. She yelled, "Victor, que tu hace?" (What are you doing) I'm not sure if she was worried because she didn't hear me or if it was her instinct, but she wanted to know, what I was up to. I replied, "Aqui calientito." I wasn't trying to hide anything; it was just a response: "I'm here, nice and warm," I replied. I didn't realize I was doing anything wrong. Then, it felt like everything slowed down. The flames started to eat away at the mattress, growing bigger by the second.

My mother must have smelled the smoke streaming from the doorway because she burst into my room and pulled me out of bed. Someone called the fire department and our neighbors started to gather in a crowd outside. I'm not sure who told my father, but he showed up furiously livid. He was enraged and hit me hard. I was terrified. My father had shaken me before when scolding me, but he never came close to hitting me before. My face was red with the first two fingers on his right hand. My neck snapped back and became stiff from the force of his hand. I was hurt mentally, physically, and emotionally. It created a new fight. My mother yelled "Tu no lo mantienes a el!" My mother's voice was loud when she told him to let me go, not touch me, and that he didn't support me financially.

My father didn't hit me like he did my mother. Although this was an isolated incident, my mother saw it as though it was going to begin a new pattern. When my father and mother fought at other times, she would yell to him, "You don't have a right to reprimand him. You don't support him. Rockefeller supports him." Rockefeller was the governor at the time so she'd reference him since we were on Welfare. It was the first time I remember getting hit by my father, and it's when my mother finally had enough. My mother was crying when she told him, "No puedo más!" (I can't take this anymore). Angry and upset, my mother grasped my hand and we left.

My mother and I shared many difficult experiences together and would feel isolated at times. I had to be strong for her.

CHAPTER 2

BLACK SHEEP

Everyone says there aren't favorites in families, but that's a lie. My relationship with most of my family was good, but it was never the best. My three aunts loved me and took care of my Mother and I, but I had a hard time clicking with my family members. It might have been because my Mother shared a lot of her life with them, so they saw everything, specifically my oldest aunt we called Titi Aida. She loved my Mother dearly. Titi Aida even named one of her daughters after my Mother. My youngest uncle, we called Tio Pipe, was very serious, but if I asked him for something he always gave it to me. They always tried to help my Mother and me when they could. However, I felt at the time that everybody's feelings came before mine. I was the black sheep.

Because my Mother was close with my aunts, my cousins felt more like brothers and sisters. We were raised to believe that family was everything and we needed to take care of each other. At one point in time or another, each of us had lived at my grandmother's apartment. We were all connected by my grandmother, who we called Mama, and had a stronger relationship because of her. Even the cousins that were younger than I am took care of me, while the cousins who were older than I am tried to take care of my father. Even with the love I felt from my aunts and cousins, I never got the same treatment my brother, Junior, did. He was definitely the favorite. You could see the difference. I know they loved me, loved us, but I still felt left out.

No one made me feel more like a Black Sheep than Mama. Junior had preference over both my Mother and me in my grandmother's apartment. It felt like the house was divided: my Mother and I versus my grandmother and Junior. Whatever the reason, my family was really disconnected. For example, if I asked my father or grandmother for something, like money, they would tell me no. Yet, if my brother didn't get what he wanted from my grandmother (Mama), he just wouldn't come home. Literally. Mama would start to worry about him and ask me to find him, "Tell Junior to come back home. I'm going to give him what he asked for." That's what stuck with me because I saw it over and over again. I was hurt because he had the upper hand; my Mother and I didn't get the treatment he got.

The separation between my grandmother and Mother could have been because my grandmother (Mama) was so independent. Mama was a Super in the building and worked in a factory. My grandmother never wanted help, and when she took help she always paid the person for it. She was a very independent woman and never wanted to depend on anyone. I even questioned my grandmother when she said she loved my Mother, because I saw things that surprised me.

One day, in my grandmother's apartment, my brother and Mama brought a box of pizza home. Getting pizza was not normal, and I remember feeling she was spoiling Junior. Mama handed him two slices of pizza, and she only gave us, my Mother and I, one piece to share. My Mother carefully cut the piece in half and picked up one side. "Oh, you took the biggest piece," I complained. My

Mother took her half slice, fresh from the oven, and hit me in the face with it. I believe she felt embarrassed by my selfish behavior so her first reaction was to correct my behavior, and hitting was her first form of discipline. I could feel the burn on my skin, searing into my cheek. With tears in my eyes, I ran to the bathroom. Mama lived in a long and narrow railroad apartment, so I had to run to the very back to get to the bathroom. With each step, I felt my face scorching more and more.

Mama and Me

My bond with my Mama was unique, but special. I was able to be open and honest with her, saying things I couldn't say to everyone else. They were afraid of disrespecting her. I was never intentionally disrespectful, but at times she would look at me and laugh at the things I told her. Appearance meant a lot to Mama, and she wanted to maintain the attitude of strength. I used to regularly sleep in her living room because there were pull out cots. Mama's room was by the front window, facing the street, and all of the other rooms fell in an almost straight line behind hers. She relaxed near that window in her room or in the living room watching Novellas (Spanish Soap Operas). Mama wasn't the type of grandmother that let us see her eating. I'm not sure if it was a sign of strength or that she wanted us to feel like she made every effort to take care of us first. Whatever the case, we didn't say much about it.

One evening I caught her eating at night, but I didn't say anything. At least, I waited until the following evening when she said, "I haven't eaten anything all day." I went up to her and said, "Mama, I saw you eating all night last night." She just looked at me and said firmly, but with a small smile, "Go lay down. Just go lay down." When my Aunts caught me talking to her like that, they told me, "You looking to get hit. Mama is going to put it on you." But Mama never hit me. She threatened it, but never did. Mama could have told my mother about how I talked to her, but she didn't. That was one of the first times I really felt like my grandmother loved me like she loved my brother Junior. Mama was hurting for me, but never told me until before she died. My whole life I never really knew how much Mama loved me until then. Mama was firm with me, because she knew I was a strong headed kid.

When I was out in the streets I started making money, which meant I also started spending money. I was making money and spending it on making myself look good. I wanted to look good, so I started spending money on my appearance. I love jewelry, and I knew a few people who gave me good deals, so I felt like I was buying it for practically nothing. You would rarely see me in a suit. Nothing like that; I dressed casually, but nice. I kept my hair long and styled too.

I went to Hair People on 56th and Lexington to get my hair styled. I paid $25, a lot of money at that time, to get my ends trimmed. I came back to Mama's house and she looked at my hair and asked, "What is that?" I smiled, "You like it? I just came from the barbershop." Mama replied in a low tone, one that let me know she wasn't happy, "What barbershop did you go to?" I was reluctant to tell her. "I paid $25 for this haircut," I mumbled. My grandmother left and headed to her room for her secret stash, a tied-up handkerchief with cash inside. Mama pulled out $25 and gave it to me. "Here's the money for your haircut," she told looking directly in my eyes. Then, Mama grabbed an additional $25 and said, "Go to a man's barbershop and get a haircut." I was upset, but knew I didn't have a choice. I didn't want to cut my hair, but if I didn't she wouldn't let me come back to stay in her house. I used the money to get my hair redone. I didn't have a choice, there was no other place to go. Even though I was angry, it reminded me that she did love me.

One of the times I was in jail for selling drugs, my father sent me a letter that said Mama needed to talk to me. I wrote back, telling him I couldn't talk to her because Mama had a block on her phone. My father responded, telling me, "That's why she told me to get in touch with you. Your grandmother took the block off her phone." I called Mama the first chance I got, and asked her for "Bendicion." She said "Dios te bendiga. Mijo tu estas bien?" (God bless you. Son are you ok?) I told her "Yeah Mama, yo estoy bien." (I am good) For one reason or another, when I called her that day and said bendicion, I finally felt like it came from her heart; that she was actually worried about me. Mama showed us all love, but she loved us all differently. Her love was unique and strict. Mama had strong opinions about me, in particular, because she knew the way I lived. I think she felt that she had to be firm with me because I grew fast and was dominate. I was a loose cannon, so Mama felt she had to control that. She saw a lot of my father in me.

Before I hung up, Mama told me she loved me. "I love you too, Mama," I responded, "but please don't tell me that I'm going to be the death of you. You always say it, and every time you do that person ends up dying. Please don't say I'm going to be the death of you." Mama was quiet for a second, and then said, "No, I asked for you to call me just to let you know that I love you." We had a strange relationship and even though she didn't say it much, we loved each other.

Months later while in jail, I was called to the medical office and received a letter stating that Mama had died. By the time I got the information it was too late to get permission to go to the funeral. I tried to see the priest to get permission to call home and he told me no that it wasn't an emergency. I lost it. The Iman, the head of the Muslims, got me permission to call home. That's when I learned I had not only missed Mama's funeral but also that my father was in the hospital because he had a heart attack.

When I got older, I realized when something bad happened to a family member Mama would tell the family not to tell me. Mama was trying to protect me, as usual, because she knew that I would react and get in trouble. I was loved by Mama, but I didn't understand her strict style and reason for her tough love at the time. This strict style felt like I wasn't being treated the same and because Mama was such an important person in my family my reaction was to feel left out, like a black sheep.

CHAPTER 3

MY MOTHER'S LOVE

Maybe my life was destined to be rough to match my mother's. Our bond was close because most of the time is was just the two of us. I called her Mami. She was a very strong woman. When Mami would get hit by my father, she would fall on the floor and look at him like, "That's all you got? Did that make you feel better?" And she was very confident, regardless of what she was going through. Mami didn't feel like she needed anybody. Yet, she was as loving as she was strong. She not only showed me love, but preached it. Mami made sure I knew never to hit a woman and only to be with someone because you love them, not because you need them. Yet, even with her strength and love, my mother spent most of her life depressed, felt humiliated at times and battled with abusive relationships. She had it worse than most people, and I had to experience it firsthand.

After Mami and father separated, we were broke. So, we stayed with a lot of different people. Mami was scared to let me out of her sight, constantly afraid she would lose me the same way she lost my brother. I was really angry at first, and the fighting and disputes taught me to trust no one. We would sleep at friend's or family's houses, never really feeling at home. Finding something to eat was difficult, but somehow my mother always had a friend who had extra. Regularly, I would hear one of her friends let her know that there was a plate of food, and my mom would always say, "Give it to my son." (*Dáselo a mi hijo*) Even though my mother struggled, my health was a priority. Once I finished, she would take the leftovers, if there were any. Mami felt she was strong enough to go a day or two without eating, but she didn't think I was able to because of my age.

When we were extremely desperate, my mother would go to welfare (Rockefeller) and ask for assistance. This was very humiliating for my mother and was always a last resort. It was a big old-fashioned brownstone on 128th Street and Park Avenue. There were a lot of offices and it was constantly busy. The workers were angry about being there, so they were disrespectful. When you went there you had to be ready to argue. The welfare workers asked you for every piece of paper, every piece of mail that you had. At that time, they sent investigators to search your house to make sure that if you said you lived alone, that you lived alone. They would even check the refrigerator to make sure you were using your food coupons the right way. If you weren't following the rules, they would cut you off immediately.

While waiting in the welfare line, my mother needed to ask for help, but her English was limited. I think the only few words she had memorized were cuss words and necessities like, "Hello," "Yes," and "No." I became Mami's translator, her interpreter. The barrier in communication infuriated her, and the things she would say would make me embarrassed. My mother must have been able to tell how ashamed I was by the pauses in my response. "Dilo como yo lo dije," (*Say it the way I said it*) was repeated like a record, and I would have to translate every cuss word to the social workers standing in front of me.

I knew my father and mother loved each other whether they were living together or not. She would find excuses to see my father again, like saying she was looking for me. Even though they were not together, my father and mother created a long-distance friendship, almost like friends with benefits, and she would go stay with him occasionally.

One day in the summer, we were in the neighborhood on 115th Street between Third and Lexington. I lived with each of them at separate times, so when they were together I wanted to be around them because it felt like we were a family again. Suddenly, I see a lady start arguing with my father. My father must have been seriously dating someone, because when he tried to hold this lady's hand she slipped past him and started arguing with my mother. My father tried to put his two cents in and the lady told him to mind his own business. Mami and the lady started hitting each other. She pulled out at razor blade and sliced my mother's legs.

It hurt to see my mother bleeding and falling to the ground, but it broke my heart to watch my father pull himself out of the picture. He didn't do anything. The lady ran away after cutting Mami, and no one attempted to stop her. My anger at my father increased. I couldn't get over the fact that they broke up because my father used to hit my mother, and now he's letting his girlfriend cut her? We moved to the Bronx.

When we moved to the Bronx, Mami had left my father and was dating someone at the time. I never knew if they were actually married, but she always called him her "husband." After Mami had been cut, we ended up staying in her sister's house until we could find an apartment. My mother met a guy while living at her sister's house and they started dating. I would like to say they got married, but I'm not sure. It didn't matter to her; she told everyone that he was her husband. They quickly moved in together to a small apartment at 480 Brooke Avenue in the Bronx, just 8 blocks away from my aunt.

My mother and her "husband" never argued in front of me, but one day I walked in and she was sobbing. My mother was hesitant, refusing to tell me what happened. I knew that he hit her. My mother was trying to hide herself. She didn't want me to look at the side of her face and tried to rush me out. It was like watching a replay of her with my father. I couldn't watch that again, not after what my father did to her. So, I went to the only other place I knew I could go back to stay with my father in Manhattan.

As strong as she was, my mother was always weak for my father. My mother would say she was looking for me so she could see my father again. I don't know what finally caused my mother to stop seeing her "husband," but she started going back around her old neighborhood and visiting old friends. One of these friends was my father, and they started talking again casually. When I saw them together I would wish that we would get back together as a family. I wanted my father to stop drinking because it was the only thing I saw that made him a bad guy and turned him into the abuser. Even after all the abuse, she never said a bad thing about my father in front of me. My Mother didn't talk bad about him because she didn't want me to hate my father. She wanted me to respect him and love him. My mother wanted me to believe that whatever they were going through was between them and that it had nothing to do with me. Although their relationship was abusive, my mother wanted me to believe that my father loved me.

The pattern of aggression and reaction continued with other guys my mother dated. After my mother broke up with her last "husband", she moved to 141st Street and Ogden Avenue with a new boyfriend. I was living with my father at the time until one of my friends decided to run away from home. I wasn't going to let my friend live on the street, so I told him I'd go with him and we went to my mother's house. We spent the night there, and in the middle of the night I heard them fighting. I was a teenager this time, and she knew I would fight anyone who hit her, so my mother tried to hide it from me. I knocked on the door and my mother responded, "Que?" (*What*). "Open the door. Open the door. Are you alright?", I said. I could hear her sobbing, "Estoy bien. Estamos discutiendo." (*I'm okay. We're just arguing, but everything's okay*) She was quieter than usual, but opened the door to let me in. I said, "Mami, is he hitting you?" With her nightgown torn and a black and blue bruise on her chest, she replied, "No el no me está dando." (*No, he's not hitting me*) I lost my mind. I couldn't handle it anymore. So, I walked out of the bedroom, to the kitchen table, where I unscrewed one of the legs. Then I went back to the bedroom to hit him with it. Mami's new boyfriend scrambled to grab a knife. In the background my mother, still concerned for him, told me "No le des en la espalda. El tiene problemas con su espalda." (*Don't hit him in the back. He has back trouble*) My friend joined me and we continued hitting him, pushing him out of the apartment and down the stairs. After this, he left and never came back, but Mami's difficult problems didn't end there.

CHAPTER 4

DIFFICULT LESSONS

Mami was tough when it came to discipline, but it was her harshness that taught me how to be independent. When I was about 10 or 11 years old, I traveled to my school, PS 51, by myself. At that time, there were pay phones inside glass booths that looked like boxes where people could put money in to make phone calls. I don't remember who taught me how to steal the change inside of these, but all I had to do was plug two wires together and the change would come out. One morning, on my way to school, I got caught stealing money from one of these booths on 149th Street and 3rd Avenue, next to a department store called Hearns. The policeman gave me a letter to give to my mother, but I couldn't convince myself to give it to her. I knew how mad she would get.

After a few weeks, there was a knock on our door. An Irish and Hispanic detective were at the door and asked, "Does Victor Muniz live here? His mother is Maria Teresa DeJesus." Mami came to the door a few moments later. "Did your son give you the letter we gave him? You were supposed to come to the precinct and you never showed up," the detective said. The Irish officer looked at us like we were crazy because we started speaking Spanish so fast and he didn't understand this at all. But the Spanish officer looked at us and said that I was going to be in a lot of trouble. He knew how our families felt at that time which was chaotic because my mother went ballistic on me and it was a rough situation. When the detectives left they were looking at each other laughing and I really believe that the Spanish officer was telling him everything that was going to happen when they left. I'm not sure if my mother understood every word he said, but it didn't matter because she knew enough to know I caused some kind of trouble. Mami was furious. She worked in a belt factory at the time, and broke two or three different belts beating my butt.

Soon after the three-belt beating, we moved to 117 East 115th, between Lexington and Park. Mami took me shopping by a grocery store near our house. I walked out of the store eating a bag of chips I grabbed while we were shopping. They might have cost a nickel, but it didn't matter once my mother noticed. "De dónde tú sacaste eso? Quien te dio eso?" *(Where did you get that from? Who gave you that?),* my mother demanded, grabbing my hand. "When we were in the store, I took it Mami," I replied. She grabbed me by my ear so hard that I started bleeding, and she pulled me back into the store. She paid the owner the nickel for the bag of chips, but he was more concerned about my ear. "No, no; It's alright, Teresa," he said when she gave him the money. This seemed to make her even more upset. "No me digas cómo criar a mi hijo," (*Don't tell me how to raise my child)* she yelled. She pulled me out of the store, never letting go of my ear.

At that time, police officers used to patrol the streets, and one stopped us after seeing my ear bleeding. He told my mother to let me go. "Que el dice," *(What did he say?)* she asked me, angrily. After I told her, she quickly said, "tell him that you came out of me and that he needs to mind his own business."

"...but Mami," I tried to negotiate with her, but it didn't work. Every time the officer said something, she would squeeze my ear tighter. By now, my blood was starting to drip down her hand because her nails were digging into my ear. I begged the officer to just leave us alone, "Don't say nothing to her. She's my mother. I'm okay. I'm okay."

But that is how it was back in the day. My mother was strict, and she would hit me for anything. If there was an elderly lady with packages in front of our stoop and I didn't offer to help, I would get hit. It was her way of teaching me respect. At the same time, if anyone tried to bully me my mother made me fight. Mami wanted me to respect myself as well, which meant standing up for myself. My first big fight was right outside of our building. I got into a fight with a boy who was much bigger than I was while we were at school. I wanted to fight him, but I didn't have a chance to win because I was so small compared to him. That day, after school, I came home and started crying out of anger. When my mother asked me what was wrong, I told her everything. She said, "Vístete. "(*Get dressed*) I was in the middle of changing out of my school clothes when I got enough courage to ask where we were going. My mother said" Pa abajo. Tú vas a pelear con el." (*Downstairs. You are going to fight him*)

I never fought anyone before, but I went downstairs and told the guy "Let's fight!" All of the buildings in New York, at that time, had steps going down to the basement because it housed the Super. There were rails at the top and a bunch of garbage cans downstairs, not too far from a fire hydrant that was raised off the ground. I could barely see over the fire hydrant if I was standing behind it. During the fight, he punched me so hard I fell, hitting my head on the fire hydrant. I was done. I didn't want to fight anymore. But that's not what my mother had in mind.

"Peleá!" *(Fight!),* she yelled, carrying a stick in her hand. I fought through tears because I was more afraid of her than I was of the bigger guy. I remembered the skills my father's boxing friend taught me, and tried my best to beat him. I landed one good punch and the guy went backwards, almost falling over the rails to the basement. Luckily, someone grabbed his feet just in time. By the end of the fight, I won, but it wasn't the kind of victory you would celebrate. I won out of fear. I remember during the fight my mother stood there with a stick and said something like," Pelea con el o te voy a dar una pela." (*You either fight him or you can get beat by me)* She was basically reminding me that," Tú *le puedes dar a él pero no me puedes dar a mi.*" *(You can hit him, but you can't hit me back)* I fought because it was better than getting a beating. I was raised not to be a bully and to respect others, but also to have respect for myself.

Looking back, it wasn't just respect for myself; I needed to have respect for elders and women as well. My mother was very strict about how elders were to be treated in our culture. If you see someone older, you should ask for the blessing "Bendicion" at all times, which meant, *It's asking for the blessing.* I got my first girlfriend at 14, and my mother showed up while we were hanging out. I said, "Bendicion, Mami," but she didn't hear me. She whipped around and smacked fire out of my face. "Que ti té crees que porqué tienes novia que no te parto la cara si haces algo mal? Que paso? No me vistes?" *(What? You think that because you have a girlfriend I won't smack you in your face if you do something wrong? What happened? You didn't see me?)* "But Mami…," I said. Then, I stopped. There was no talking back, it was useless. Parents said what they said and that was it.

Mami not only had to deal with trying to raise me on her own but the difficulties with relationships and providing during that time was overwhelming. We were desperate at that time and Mami became very depressed and even suicidal. When I came home one day, I found my mother with her wrists cut. This was the first time she tried to commit suicide. I had to call the ambulance to get her, but thankfully she didn't go deep enough to cause serious damage. Another time, she mixed peroxide, bleach, and other chemicals and drank them. I caught her, and called the ambulance again. They pumped her stomach in the hospital. The third time Mami was on the roof ready to jump and I begged her not to do this to me. I was in the house watching TV when I noticed she wasn't there. I went to search for her and the first place I went to was the roof. At the time I wasn't sure what drew me to go there first, but there she was, ready to jump. When my mother saw me coming it was like she saw a ghost. I believe that because I caught her, she didn't want to see me suffer. I believe she tried to kill herself because of the life she was living. I really believe that my presence was what kept her from jumping. Mami loved me too much and knew it would be too traumatizing. It isn't the lesson she would want me to learn. She was more concerned for me than for herself.

After that attempt, Mami stopped trying to kill herself.

CHAPTER 5

MY MOTHER'S ILLNESS

Until 1970, my mother was always there for me. In the spring of 1970, my mother was living in the Bronx on Ogden Avenue, when she told me that she was feeling sick. Her neighbor and I took her to the Metropolitan hospital. My Mother was diagnosed with lung cancer there. Even though she had tried to commit suicide three times in a row, I could tell she wasn't ready to die. Although my mother never said it, she didn't have to; I knew that she wanted to make sure I was alright before she passed. I was 16 years old when my mother got sick.

That spring of 1970, my father was living with another woman, who I treated like a mother and even called, "Mom". She was someone from the same neighborhood where I was raised, and took care of me. Mom took care of everyone. My father's girlfriend (Mom) worked at the hospital where my mother was diagnosed with cancer, and she made it a priority on her time off to visit my mother. I thought it might make my mother mad or jealous, but she seemed relieved. My mother told Mom, "Cuida a Víctor como si fuera tú hijo." (*I want you to take care of Victor as if he was yours*) Even though Mom was only a few years older than I was, she promised my mother she would. Some stress seemed to leave my mother, and she told Mom, "No te preocupes de Júnior. Yo me lo voy a llevar conmigo." (*Don't worry about his brother. I'm taking him with me*) In fact, my brother was killed three years later.

The doctors argued about if she was ready to leave, but ended up releasing my mother from the hospital on April 13, 1970. Part of the reason why the doctors didn't agree about my mother being discharged was because her surgeries left her with a hole under her arm on her right side. It was there to drain some of the blood and pus where they removed the tumors. When she left the hospital, Mami weighed around 60 pounds. Mom warned her, "Don't go home. You don't have anyone to attend to you. You need to change the patches on your side and make sure you take your medicine." Mom offered to take care of my mother. Mom said, "You can stay with me and Jorge." My mother responded, "No yo no me puedo quedar contigo. Jorge vive contigo. Yo no me puedo quedar en tu cama?" (*No, I won't stay there because Jorge's living with you. What do I look like sleeping in his bed?*) Mom looked at her and said, "If anyone could sleep in his bed, it should be you. You're the mother of his kids." It was enough to convince my mother to stay with them for two days, but she was determined to leave after. My mother kept saying that she needed to go home since it was check day and she had to pay her rent and bills.

I went to my father's place to pick Mami up, and I was able to easily carry my mother down the stairs. She was so light. I put her in a cab and went home with her, but I could tell that my mother wasn't going to live long while she was there. Her neighbor came to visit, and told my mother, "Quieres café negro?" (*I'm so happy to see you. Do you want some black coffee?*) My mother responded, "Si pero dame un poquito. No cómo le sirves a tu esposo." (*Yeah, but just give me a little bit. Not a lot like you give your husband*). The neighbor jokingly answered, "Te voy a dar mucho para que duermas mucho." (*I'm going to give you a lot so you can sleep a lot*) It was the first sign of many that my mother wouldn't make it very long.

The next morning, I ran errands for my mother, making sure all the bills were paid. I sat Mami in a chair and went to make her bed, tucking in the corners the same way my Mom showed me, making sure that each edge included a hospital corner fold. "Tú estás haciendo esa cama como si fuera la última vez que voy a dormir en esa cama," (*You're making that bed so good, like it's going to be the last time I sleep in that bed*) my mother told me. That night, I slept in the bed with Mami. It was hard to sleep. I couldn't stop focusing on the hole in her side and I could tell she was in pain. It's as if looking at her caused her even more discomfort, and the morphine that the doctors gave her didn't take away all the agony. Around 3:00 that morning, I felt my mother's weight on me. She was trying to kiss me. I started yelling her name, "Mami, wake up! Mami, wake up, please." I tried to move her. Nothing. Finally, I touched the hole and she stayed still. The hole felt like death. Before this moment, I couldn't even stand close to my mother on that side without her jumping in pain. When she didn't even flinch, I knew my mother had died. I really believe that if I had woken a moment earlier, I would have felt her lips on my cheek. Her last movement was to kiss me goodbye. My mother passed on April 17, 1970.

When my mother passed, I lost it. I sobbed. I ran to the neighbor, and she called the police. The morgue was backed up, so we had to wait for hours. I was sick. I needed heroine. I had the money, but I didn't know anyone I could buy from since I was in The Bronx. Desperate for drugs, I told the police, "I'll be right back." I jumped in a cab and headed to Manhattan. I was angry every time the cab stopped, and finally I couldn't take it anymore. I gave the driver a few dollars and jumped out of the cab. I ran across the Third Avenue Bridge into Manhattan because I could get there faster on foot than he could drive.

I was running down Lexington Avenue and realized I had to stop in Barcelona to tell my father and Mom that my mother died. My father looked at me with doubt, but then he saw how red my eyes was from crying. I ran to my grandmother's apartment to find my brother, but I stopped on 110th street and Lexington first. I knew I could get drugs there.

When I got to my grandmother's apartment, I saw my brother down the street with one of his friends. I didn't really know how to tell him, so I mumbled, "We lost Mami. We don't have a mother." My brother grabbed me by the arms and shook me. "Stop playing with me like that,"

Junior yelled. His friend calmly said, "Look at him. He doesn't look like he's playing. He's a bundle of nerves. Just look at him." My brother broke down then, crying. Junior came back to The Bronx with me.

They had police in front of my mother's door, watching over her. The overload in the city morgue was worse than we expected, and it actually took them a few days to pick up my mother's body. Mom and my father made the funeral arrangements, and the last time I saw my mother was during the viewing in the Gonzalez Funeral Home on 109th Street and Madison.

CHAPTER 6

A FATHER ENRAGED

I get my temper from my Father. I'm not proud of it, but it grew from watching how he treated my mother. Even when they didn't live together, he would still come around to see me. It was never a question if they loved each other. I knew they did. They just couldn't live together.

When I was young, I had to watch my father hit my mother. I couldn't fight my father. I wasn't strong enough. I wouldn't be able to stop him, and I knew that. But, I still tried. I remember being young and grabbing my father, ready to punch, but he simply pushed my face away. I knew I couldn't win, but more than anything I just wanted him to acknowledge that I was there and to stop. But he didn't stop. He never stopped. My father kept beating my mother, so my hatred kept growing.

My rage started to build more and more the longer they interacted. I remember being furious when my father's girlfriend cut my mother with razor blades. Watching my father do nothing while my mother kicked and tried to get away destroyed me. Watching my mother go through that situation wasn't what hurt the most. The people who were around held me down while my mother was getting cut. No one helped her. I can still hear her screaming and gasping for air, and all I could think about was if she was going to live. No one there defended her, and all I could do was cry. It broke my heart, and I held on to that pain for a long time. I was furious with everyone, especially my father's girlfriend. After the fight was over, I ran to the store and bought some lye. I tracked down my dad's girlfriend and threw the lye in her face. I cried because I was angry and driven to harm her.

It was a long time before I saw anyone stand up to my father. One day, he decided to come to my grandmother's (Mama's) apartment. I was about 8 years old, and I could smell that he had been drinking. My father always had a gun on him, and Mama didn't allow guns in her house. That day, she had enough. She looked him straight in the eye and said, "Que yo te dicho?! Yo no quiero revólveres en mi casa." (*What have I told you? I don't want guns in my house. Don't bring guns in my house*). My father slammed the gun on top of the shelf and told her, "si tu no fuera mi madre te pegaba un tiro." (*If you weren't my mother, I'd blow your brains out*) Mama just looked at him and said, "Oh si?" (*Oh, yeah...?*) She took off running towards the kitchen, grabbed an old black iron skillet and started to run towards him. When Mama got close enough, she started beating him with the skillet. She chased him around, beating him and yelling, "Méteme el Tiro? Me vas a tirar un tiro!?" (*So... you gonna shoot me!?*) It reminded me of how he used to beat my mother, and I couldn't help but laugh while my father finally got his.

Even after this, I still had so much anger built up towards my father. After seeing him fight with another woman, I muttered, "One day, I'll be big and we will confront each other." I don't know if he heard me, but it was like I made a promise to myself.

That day didn't come until I received a furlough from jail and headed home. No one expected me. I was hot from some conflicts and beef in the block, so I went and got a gun from one of my friends to protect myself. I placed the gun in the back of my hip, right in the waistband to keep it secure. I went to look for my wife at the time, but I couldn't find her, so I went to my father's house instead. I could smell the weed and crack from outside. I knocked on the door, and heard my father say, "Who?". I responded that it was me, and I could hear him tell the people inside, in a panicked voice, "It's my son! It's my son!" I could smell the crack burning inside, and the frantic noises inside let me know that he was trying to hide the drug use from me

When my father opened the door, I said, "How you doing Papi, Bendicion." Seeing him with the drugs meant nothing to me. I was just happy to be home for seven days. I asked him if he had seen my wife, and he grew angry. "Ah, she's just like your mother... a street girl", he responded. I lost it. I left, crying tears of frustration and anger. While going down stairs, I bumped into his wife at the time. I called her Mom because of how caring she was. I told her what happened, and she sighed. "I can't take it no more. I think this is the time. He's going to have to give me some respect," I exclaimed. "My Mami is already dead. Why is he still talking negatively about her?"

Mom could hear the pain in my voice. "Victor, don't do nothing stupid," she said. "No. I'm going to do it. I've had enough. This is breaking my heart. I've had enough." Mom could tell the anger in my voice was different than before. She seemed concerned and said, "I'll be back. Wait for me, Nene." That's the nickname used to make me feel comforted, but not this time. After she left, I snapped.

My father came downstairs and I started arguing with him instantly. I'd never actually gotten into an argument with him before. The child in me screamed about how much he hurt my mother, how much he hurt me. I relived it in my mind. Before I knew it, I had punched my father. As soon as I punched him, my heart broke. I heard his nose crack and was sure I broke his nose. He started bleeding immediately. Blood poured down his lips and chin. I just wanted treat him the way he treated hit my mother. No, it was more than that. I wanted to fight for my mother, since she was never able to. I wanted to stand up for Mami.

A few of his friends jumped in to stop me, but I reached to the back of my hip grabbed the gun. I yelled at them not to get in the way, to leave me alone. "You didn't stop him when he used to hit my mother!", I yelled. "This is between me and my father!" They backed away, and I kept holding the gun until I felt like they were a safe distance. Even with the weight of the gun in my hands, the crazy part was that I didn't actually want to shoot him. I just wanted him to feel the same pain he caused my mother all those years. While I was realizing this, his friends grabbed him and told him to go upstairs and get cleaned up.

While my father was upstairs, I could hear the commotion of him in the bathroom while he talked to his friends. My father wanted to fight me. He was ready to do whatever he had to. One of his friends clearly said, "Jorge, I don't advise you to go downstairs. Your son has so much rage right now he could probably kill you with his bare hands."

When I realized he wasn't coming down, I went outside and sat in front of the building on East 115th Street, next to a fire hydrant. I cried like I had never cried before. I was ashamed, angry, proud, justified. "Mami, that was for you," I thought. I didn't know what to do now. At this point, being in jail felt better than where I was. The happiness of the furlough disappeared into the air. Mom saw me crying, and nervously asked "Nene (*Baby*), what did you do?" I told her everything. "It'll be alright," she told me while wrapping me in her arms. "Everything will be alright."

My father and I stopped talking to each other for a while after that. No words, whatsoever. Once the furlough was over, I went back to jail. I didn't get out again until they let me go on a work release 7 and 0, which meant 7 days at home and no days to sleep in, since I had to work. I would report to work and see my counselor once a week.

Even though time passed, the rage never left. While I was on 7 and 0, I got into a fight with a guy named Chino who disrespected my wife, at the time. We were sitting in a car and I heard him say something to my wife, at the time. "Did Chino disrespect you?" I asked. She told me no, but I knew something was wrong. "You sure Chino didn't say nothing to you? Don't avoid it, because it's going to keep happening." I was direct. "Yeah," she confided, "he said, 'Ahi esta la mujer del guapo.'" (*There's the wife of the tough guy*) I instantly starting walking toward him.

I was outnumbered, since Chino had a friend with him, but that didn't stop me. I had arguments with Chino in the past and warned him that if he ever disrespected her, it would be personal. I told him to swing at me if he saw me again because I wasn't coming to talk. So, this time, when I walked toward him, I expected him to take a shot at me. When I got close, Chino swung at me, but I was prepared. I reached back, pulled out a knife, and swung at him. Chino's friend went to jump in, and out of the corner of my eye I could see a group of guys from his block coming at me towards the left. I looked at the right towards a way out, and saw my father coming with a stick to defend me.

At that moment, our argument in the past was instantly over. There was no apology for what he did or what I did. It just ended. After that incident, my father and I had the relationship I imagined when I was a kid.

CHAPTER 7

FAMILY ISN'T ALWAYS BLOOD

I started getting close to the woman my father was living with when my mother got sick. I called her Mom and she was someone from the neighborhood where I was raised. Mom worked as a nurse, and it fit her because she was very nurturing. I started really trusting Mom when she would make it her business to go and take care of my biological mother (Mami) when she had her cancer diagnosis. Even on her days off, Mom would visit Mami in the hospital. I didn't feel like many people stood up for Mami, so Mom became someone I looked up to and respected. Having Mom around helped me and Mami feel more relieved.

Mom was only a few years older than I was, but she agreed to take care of me when Mami asked her to. I enjoyed being around her. I'd tell her, "I'll be right back," steal a stash from a dealer or do a quick stick up, then come back to her with the money. We would go see movies or get something to eat with the money I got. We would walk down the street talking and laughing, but I always had to keep an eye out. I was wanted in a lot of places, so our trips were dangerous. I'd have to regularly tell her, "Oh no, let's go through here" or "No, let's go through there." Sometimes we'd just end up going down a street where I was wanted because I felt safe with her. I knew she had my back. Mom made me feel secure at all times. I felt safe with her like you do with loving biological mother. Because that's what mother's do.

Mom was my supporter, my go-to girl. Anything I was uncomfortable with or was going to do, I used to talk to her about it. One day I told Mom about some money I stole from my boss because my father didn't want to give me any money. Mom fixed it. It was my welfare money.

Mom went to my father and got the money then paid my boss back. I was surprised that the boss forgave me. I was blessed and didn't know it. I felt comfortable telling her when I did bad things because she would be there for me regardless.

Mom never turned her back on me when I did something wrong. She taught me what it meant to love unconditionally. But I didn't only go to her for the bad things. Mom was there for me for the positive changes I wanted to make in my life as well. Every time I wanted to stop using drugs, she encouraged me to get in a program. Mom never gave up regardless of how many times. Unlike some of my family members, Mom would be there for me 150% and encourage me, give me advice and explain my options. She never gave up on me like she knew I was going to change. Mom always believed in me and somehow, she knew that it was just a matter of time.

CHAPTER 8

JUNIOR'S DEATH

When my mother was about to pass she made plans for someone to take care of me, but she didn't do the same for my brother. "Don't worry about Junior. I'm taking him with me," she said. Three years and 1 month after my mother's death, my brother was killed.

During the beginning of the 1970s, my brother went missing. It was normal for my brother to disappear, he did it regularly. At that time, we were both in and out of jail so when he was in jail at least we knew where he was.

The year Junior went missing, I had a furnished room on 115th Street between 3rd and Lexington, and I was just about to get married to my first wife. I was hustling, like normal, when I heard Junior came around looking for me. My father said, "Your brother was looking for you. He didn't talk to me. He just said he needed to talk to you." My father told me that Junior stood there for a while, waiting for me, but left after a while. That was the last time anyone saw my brother.

Three days later, detectives came to my grandmother's apartment and told us that Junior was killed. I was asked to identify the body. I was angry. I felt so guilty accountable for his death and it hit me hard. I couldn't stop thinking about his last moments. Junior was looking for me. Would he still be alive if he had found me?

Losing Junior was a big hit to our family. He was the first grandchild, my only brother, my father's oldest son. I took Juniors death exceptionally hard. Three years before, my mother died in my arms after kissing my cheek. Now, my brother was dead and I could have possibly stopped it. The guilt intensified. I thought it was all my fault. I should have been there to save his life. I was supposed to be there. Or maybe I would have known who had killed him.

Within a few days, the detectives told us they had an idea who killed Junior, but they didn't have enough evidence. They thought the murderer was the same person who had killed three guys before, but they didn't have enough proof. The evidence they did have was his body. Junior was stabbed 17 times and thrown in a dumpster during a rainstorm. It took them 3 or 4 days to find the body, and it had rained during most of those days. When the police found Junior, there wasn't a single drop of blood in his body. His body was decomposed, and the autopsy didn't show that he was drunk or high. In fact, he was unrecognizable, but I noticed his tattoo. I was able to identify him by that. Junior was 21 when he died.

The police told us about who they thought committed the crime, even though they doubted it was just one person. They believed that the guy who killed my brother was a self-styled minister who was gay. He came from down south, Atlanta, Georgia, and had already killed 3 kids they knew of. They believed that my brother was the oldest of the victims. My family were outraged, devastated. We couldn't believe it. We thought it was impossible. How could something like this happen to us?

Months later, the suspect was caught after committing another murder. I was able to speak with the detectives when they came to my grandmother's apartment to tell us the good news: "We caught the guy who killed Jorge Muniz. He will never go home again." The detectives told us as much as they could. The detectives were on his tail. He killed another kid right after my brother and that's when they arrested him. They finally had the proof they needed. The killer confessed to the murders and when the judge asked him if he felt any remorse, he said "If they lived again, I'd kill them again." The detectives classified the murders as "passion killings." The killer claimed that the kids he killed, including my brother, were kids he fell in love with but they didn't love him back. So, he killed them. The detectives weren't even sure if there were more bodies of those he killed while he traveled from Atlanta to New York.

I was devastated. I couldn't understand why it took so long to find the truth. The guilt and anger leaked into my personal life. When I was arrested and got into legal trouble, it seemed like it would be easiest to say, "I'm guilty." I'd always say, "It's mine your honor." I plead guilty for what I did and also sometimes whatever they wanted to charge me with, because I wanted to run into the killer in prison, and get the chance to get revenge for my brother. I spent a large part of my life being angry and vengeful about my brother's murder.

My brother's death made me reflect on his protective nature, my past, and also shaped my future. I realized how helpless I was as a kid and how much I was reacting to anger. I couldn't protect my mother from my father because I was too small. I couldn't protect my mother from cancer. I couldn't protect my brother from being murdered. The guilt and anger lived in me and ate away at me. I was the man of the house; It was my job to protect the family. My motto became, "If you touch my family, you touch me!"

CHAPTER 9

BEING A MAN

I always thought being a man meant doing what you have to do to protect your family, by any means necessary. "If you touch my family, you touch me!" Depending on how you were raised, protection by any means doesn't necessarily mean anything crazy. To provide protection requires responsibilities, like working, loving, and teaching. I felt like fighting for my family was one of those responsibilities.

I learned what it meant to be a man around the age of 8. It was back in the day, back when they still put bottles of milk in front of people's houses. The bread man left the bread in front of the stores. Mami and I moved to 335 East 118th Street, between Second and First Avenues. It was a rough area. There were a lot of neighborhood street gangs, but they all seemed to get along with us. At least, they did for some time. I don't know what happened, but it changed quickly.

One day someone knocked on our door. When Mami answered, around 5 or 6 guys from one of the local gangs were waiting at our door. The men asked her to make them some coffee. I could see that they had taken the bread from the storefront and had gotten milk from someone's doorstep. Mami agreed to make them some coffee. They were sitting around, drinking the coffee and enjoying themselves, when everything changed. The gang members started surrounding her looking at her lustfully being fresh. The men started grabbing her, molesting her. I knew they were going to rape her. Nervously, I ran out to the fire escape. I knew I couldn't fight them. I was an expert at running up and down the fire escape because back in the day that's what we did; jump roofs and go up and down fire escapes. So, I knew the perfect time to let the ladder down and start climbing down to the street. I heard one of them yell, "We gotta go! We gotta go! He's going to call the police." As I looked down, I saw them running out of the building.

I quickly started climbing back up to check on Mami. I scrambled into the window and ran straight toward where I left her. "They didn't get to do anything to me," Mami reassured me. But it was my first taste of what life would be like living alone with her after she broke up with my father and I had to be the man of the house. Providing and protecting were my two main tasks I thought.

I need to learn to provide so I was shining shoes at the time. I thought I was helping Mami by bring in more money. I charged 15 cents a shine back then. My father started to work with the Italians, collecting numbers, and they were the best customers. When I went to see him, they would give me five dollars for a shine, which was a lot of money at that time. Every cent I earned went to Mami. I wanted to be the man of the house, to provide money for her when we needed it.

One day, Mami and I were walking down 116th Street and 3rd Avenue looking at the stores. We went by one store and I saw the perfect outfit. It was completely white and even had white Decks- White sneakers, tennis shoes. Today they look like Vans. I gazed at it, telling my mother, "Wow, that is a nice outfit. Whenever I work I'm going to buy myself an outfit like that." Mami said slyly, "Why don't you buy it?" I laughed, "Mami, I don't have any money." She smiled and said, "Nene, why don't you go home and go to the drawer and look under the clothes. There's some money." Every cent I earned and had given to help Mami, she ended up saving for me. Even when we needed stuff in the house, Mami didn't use the money I gave her. She kept it all for me.

Protecting the Family

A few years later, my mother broke up with a guy she was dating and we moved to 141st and Willis Avenue. I was visiting her at the time and she was playing dominoes in the neighborhood. One of the guys at the table spoke disrespectfully to her, and I couldn't handle it. I flipped the domino table and started arguing with him. My mother told me, "No, no," trying to make sure I didn't start anything. There was a rumor that I was in a gang, and she knew it. The guy angrily said, "Yeah, you're a tough guy. You're gonna get yours," before leaving. I went back to my father's house in Manhattan and told him everything that happened. I told him the truth: how this guy disrespected Mami, how I responded, what the guy said. My father got a couple of his boys, and I got a couple of my boys. We headed back to her neighborhood.

I was a fighter, like my father, and he had a plan. My father told me, "Walk by yourself and see if they're going to hit you." My boys walked behind me at a distance and my father and his boys were on the other side of the street. The guy that had disrespected my mother wasn't there, but the other people who were playing dominoes were. My father warned the people who were there, "If something happens to Teresa, we'll be back and we won't be talking." My mother saw me with my father, and she begged me to let it go. "I have to stay living here," she pleaded. "No!", I thought. "You gotta move outta here," I told her, about to leave, "I'll come check on you." The next day, one of the guy's friends came up to me and said, "Listen, I spoke to him and all that. This don't need to get out of control." Even though it was squashed, I kept encouraging my mother to move because I was worried the guy would react and take it out on her. Eventually, she finally did move to Ogden Avenue. I felt like I was able to protect her, even if it was just a little. This protective attitude extended to the rest of my family as well.

I was a little older than my cousins, but I was still close to them. One of my aunts had a boyfriend, and during a fight with my aunt, he broke the private door downstairs to get to her. My grandmother kicked him out, but I found out that he threatened my little cousins and hit my aunt. After seeing how my father treated my mother, I was enraged. I walked up to my cousins and tried to comfort them saying, "You're going to be alright. I promise. You keep going to school. Don't be afraid; I'm going to always be around you. You won't always see me, but I'm there. Go to school like normal."

After talking to my cousins, I told one of my friends what happened. He said, "Okay. Let me go change clothes." My friend came back dressed like he was going hunting. He even brought paint to put on his face. He was crazy. "What are you doing?!" I asked, puzzled. My friend responded coldly, "No! We gotta get this guy. He can't threaten our family!" By his response and the look in his eyes, I could tell he saw me like his brother.

We went to my grandmother's apartment, and I told her that everything was going to be alright. "Don't worry about nothing. Ain't nothing going to happen to your grandkids or your daughter," I told her calmly and protectively. My grandmother was a strong woman, and simply responded, "What are you going to do?" My grandmother kept looking at my friend. I told her we weren't going to do anything, but she wasn't convinced. "Don't get in no trouble. Don't do nothing stupid," she warned. "We're not going to do nothing," I responded, "but nobody can mistreat my family."

My friend and I kept surveillance like cops do. We watched over my cousins, but also kept an eye on everything moving in the neighborhood. After a few days, I noticed a car that my Aunt's boyfriend was in following us while I was walking with my cousins. I got them home safely, and went to my friend's van which was parked about a block away, next to the eye doctor's office on 108th and 3rd. Another one of my cousins started walking down the street and I watched as he dropped his radio, ready to fight whoever was in the suspicious car. My friend saw my cousin's reaction, and he got excited. Before I knew it, my friend opened the door of the van and started running towards my cousin and towards the conflict. I didn't have a choice but to jump out of the van and follow. We chased my aunt's ex-boyfriend on foot all the way to 106th street. I kept screaming while we were running, yelling about how he had hit a woman. I planned to take all my frustrations and anger out on this guy. I was fully prepared to fight to protect my family. Unfortunately, he got away but the message was out there. People knew not to mess with my family.

After my grandmother, Mama, found out about that incident, she used to tell everyone not to tell me if conflict happens with them. "Don't tell Victor," was the phrase. It didn't stop anything; I always found out. Like when my grandmother was alone in the house with my oldest uncle. He used to drink a lot, and some guys had followed him upstairs. They started pushing him, but Mama stayed calm. She went into her bedroom to grab a gift from under the bed. Mama had always kept gifts that she was given but never used underneath her bed. Mama took one gift after another and offered them to the guys.

They weren't happy with the gifts, and one of the guys told Mama to, "Get up on that bed." She looked at them and calmly asked, "What are you going to do to me? I could be your mother. I could be your grandmother." They didn't respond, so she said firmly, "You better hurry up and go because my son and grandson are on their way here. I advise you to leave." By the time my father and I got there, they had left. But right after she told us what happened, my father and I immediately ran down the stairs and split up to search for them. We never found those guys who almost assaulted my grandmother. We came back to ask my grandmother for more details and a description but she refused. Mama didn't want us to get into trouble.

Where we came from, I had to learn how to protect my family by any means necessary. I had to learn early how to be strong and survive whatever came my way and I did it with toughness.

CHAPTER 10

SURVIVAL

I've been blessed to celebrate my 65th birthday on September 8th 2018. Which means I remember the '60's and 70's well. I had grown up, had my own life and place, and became a drug addict myself at the age of 13. (More on that story in Chapter 12, The Drug Game). During this time, I was going back and forth between my mother's house, my father's house, my grandmother's apartment and even sleeping on rooftops and basements.

I always said if somebody was going to do something to me or kill me, I didn't want them to catch me sleeping. I always felt I had to be prepared and able to defend myself. It may sound crazy, but there were a few times where I slept on the roof or on the bottom floor, just to make sure I was safe. But that wasn't enough; I went to extremes. I would handcuff myself to the banister when I was on the roof. That way if someone did show up and wanted to throw me off, they would have to wake me up or find a way to get the keys. That was always my mentality.

I used to shine shoes on 149th and Third Avenue across the street from Hearns Department Store. An older white man stopped in front of my shoeshine box and told me, "I have so many shoes for you to shine, but I can't bring them all out here." I was excited about the potential cash, so I asked him "What do you want to do?" His response was to ask, "Can you come to my house?" I told him I could, and got into his car. I watched out the window while he was driving and noticed we had entered La Playita de los Mojones *(Hunts Point)*. The car slowed to a stop in an open space of land, about half a while away from where supposed to go. We were in an alley, somewhat out of sight, and before I could ask why we stopped he started to touch my leg. This guy was trying to take advantage of me.

Quickly realizing what this was, I told him "I have to pee really bad." I didn't act afraid. He stared at me really hard, and after a few seconds, he said, "Fine. Go pee behind the car. Look at where you are, though. If you run, I will catch you." Innocently, I muttered "Okay," and opened the car door. I went behind the car and acted like I was peeing, when in reality I was trying to see if I could run fast enough to make it to the bar. It seemed pretty far, and there was a decent sized lot I would have to run through before I could reach it. I started to get second thoughts about trying to run, and realized that I had been outside the car too long already. I stepped back into the car and he started to touch my leg more aggressively, grabbing at my penis. I knew I had to do something.

"I have to poop," I blurted. Pretending to pee worked, so maybe this would too. He looked at me skeptically. I didn't know what to expect as he moved his hand off my leg and started to reach upwards. His hand slowly backed away from me, and went into the glove compartment. He took out some paper and grunted, "go behind the car, but remember what I told you. It's useless to run." I opened the door, went behind the car, started to pull down my pants, and lowered my body like I was going to poop. Then I ran. I made a break for the bar as fast as I could. I could hear the engine of his car starting behind me, which only made my legs move faster. I started to scream, "I need to use a phone! I need to use a phone! This man kidnapped me!" hoping that someone in the bar could hear me.

And somehow, they did. There were a few men that ran outside. I could hear them telling the bartender go get to the phone. As I got closer to them, the car caught up to me. That man must have seen all of the guys from the bar headed toward me, because as I looked back I saw him turn around to leave. Within a few minutes, the police came to take me home. They told my mother what happened, and she scolded me at first. Mami told me that I knew better than to get in that car, but then she hugged me tightly and told me how much she loved me. Mami warned me to stay alert when I was out in the streets. She said I needed to watch my back at all times.

Surviving in the Streets

But the streets became my home. My friends used to make fun of me when I sold drugs. They claimed I wasn't built to be a dealer because I was too easy or too good to people. Maybe I decided I would look out for those who couldn't look out for themselves. I'm not sure if it was the right or wrong way, but a lot of the guys spent their money with me buying drugs instead of taking care of their own homes.

Even the hard-working guys would earn credit, then come Friday and pay me to get some while hiding the drugs from their wives. They would disappear for a while, because they wouldn't have the money to pay for their bills and things like that. Sometimes their wives would come to me and say, "Hey Victor, have you seen my husband?" I'd always tell them, "No. He was around earlier" or "He came around and then left." Some would start crying, complaining that they didn't know what they were going to do. I'd always ask them what the problem was, or if they were okay. "No, the baby don't have no milk and there's nothing to eat" was a common response, so I'd take the wife to the store on 115th Street and Lexington and say, "get what you need." I'd pay for them each time.

I used to buy my customers' wives' groceries, which got me in a few disagreements. The wives would eventually tell their husbands, "If it wasn't for Victor, our kids wouldn't eat." The husbands would get mad at me, and they would ask their wives, "why don't you just go stay with Victor, then?" The worst was when it would happen in front of me. I'd ask them to keep me out of it, but that rarely worked. My father said these situations were going to be the death of me. I'd always try to reassure the guys, tell them "Listen to me, B. You don't have to worry about your wife doing anything with me or anything like that. Because that's not the type of guy I am. I wouldn't do that. But the reality is, B, I'm not going to leave your kids without no food".

The husbands, who were my customers, would play hard in front of their wives. But as soon as their wives left, they would thank me and tell me that I didn't know how much it meant to them to buy food for their wives and kids. My friends would always tell me that I was getting played. They would say that these guys were just getting high for free because they knew I would end up paying for the groceries and milk with the money they'd given me earlier to pay off their credit. I'd tell my friends that I didn't care, "Play me or not, who got the money? Who is making the money? It's their money. So even if I buy the babies milk and their wives' food to eat, I got more profit from them. Why be greedy?" I convinced myself it was better to be the giving guy than the greedy guy. I helped them survive, and I survived off of them.

CHAPTER 11

MY PRIDE AND JOY

In the late 70's I starting going out with this young girl named Liz, who became pregnant with my first child. So, we wound up getting married quickly. I was clubbing one night, and when I came home to go to bed, my wife asked me, "What are you doing?" I told her I was going to sleep, and she looked at me strangely. Liz was direct and said, "I'm in labor." I was high out of my mind from smoking, but I knew I had to take her to the hospital. Getting high was comfortable and easy. The drugs made me feel more secure, more careful. So, I was ready to go.

When we got to the hospital, they told me to take my wife back home, walk around some, and bring Liz back when the contractions were closer. We walked all morning and I took her back to the hospital after the contractions were closer together as suggested.

My son, Victor Jr., was born September 9, 1979. A day after my own birthday. As a Puerto Rican it's a tradition to name your firstborn son after you to have a namesake. The birth of my firstborn son was a rude awakening.

This new event was a reality check. I had to do something to take care of a new life, but that was easier said than done. I was an addict and sold drugs to make a living. I felt like I needed to change, to be better for him, but I needed the money to take care of him. I knew that I had to try to be a better dad. I stopped using heroin, but kept smoking lots of weed and sniffing coke. I snorted so much cocaine that I had a hole from the inside of my nose to the other and it would bleed like crazy. Although I didn't want to be there anymore, I couldn't leave the streets.

This caused even more strain on my relationship with my son's mother. Liz and I were already having difficulties. Because she was so young that money problems only made it worse. And we didn't realize how much it costs to raise a kid. The stress made it difficult to maintain a relationship. So, I was on and off with Liz, but I spent most of the time in jail. Sometimes the more you make in the game, the more you want. And while I wanted to be with my son all the time, it wasn't good while I was running in the streets. I sold drugs and had people under me selling, so I was always up and down spending time and taking care of my son. It felt like I was always playing catch-up and couldn't make enough money.

Of course, sometimes parents do the wrong things. I thought I was doing the right things by buying Victor Jr. the best clothes and everything he wanted. He was a little me. But I spent little time with Victor Jr. because I spent much of his childhood in jail. And while I was in different prisons, Victor Jr. grew quickly to follow the footsteps that I set for him.

My Son in the Game

My son saved me once. I was selling drugs and he came into the block and jumped on me, yelling, "Papi! Papi! Don't do nothing." At the time, I didn't have a grip on the reality; he was way more advanced to the drug game than I thought even at 11 years old. "Papi! Don't sell nothing. They watching you," he cried. I asked, "What are you talking about?" and I started to look around. I quickly realized there were two police officers sitting on the roof, watching me. I laid low and waited for the guy who was selling for me to come around. "Yo, Victor, you gotta pay me. I worked so many hours," he said while walking up to me. "I'm not paying you nothing," I responded. "I was about to get arrested and you weren't doing your job. You wasn't paying attention. The one I gotta pay is my son. He saved my life."

That experience should have opened my eyes to a bigger pattern, but it didn't. One day my son asked me for a couple of dollars while I was waiting for a shipment to sell. I told him, "I don't have no money now. I'll give you some later." He looked at me puzzled and said, "How come you don't have no money? You know Jack over there has a lot of money and he owes you." I blurted, "What do you mean? Jack got what money?" I quickly got dressed and left the house, bringing my son along. I walked straight up to Jack and said, "Where's my money?" Confused, Jack responded, "Victor, I don't have no money." My son looked at me and said, "Papi, he's lying to you." Enraged, I punched Jack in the face and he fell to the floor. I grabbed my knife and held it to his throat. My son started sobbing and then screaming, "Papi! Don't do it! Don't do it!" His voice is what made me stop. I looked at Jack and said, "You know what? I'm not going to cut you. My son saved your life. He don't want me to do that to you." My son, listening, came out and said, "I didn't save his life. I saved yours. The police was going by. But they passed already. Do what you gotta do. You can stab him now." At that moment my heart broke. Seeing my son think this way opened my eyes. I had to be better.

I tried to change. I even turned myself in around 1987 after I spent Christmas with my son, but I just continued to go in and out of jail. One of the times I came home, I went to his mother's house to find my son, but nothing was there. I couldn't even find my clothes. My son's mother, Liz, had gotten a transfer to move to Brooklyn into the Bronxville Projects on Mother Gadsen and Dumont. When I found out where Liz was, I went to visit them both. It was a rough area. When I walked in, some kids were in the downstairs part of the building. "Oh, you're Victor's father? Your name is Victor?" they asked. These kids were from the hood and they were stick up kids, drug dealers. I was very upset. "Who are you? I don't even know you," I mumbled, pushing past them. I knocked on the door angrily and demanded to know where Victor Jr. was when Liz opened the door. "Who are these people? How do they know my name?" I demanded.

"Victor told them that his father was coming home and things were going to change," his mother responded, then finally told me Victor Jr. was downstairs. So, I rushed to get him.

I found out that Victor Jr. and his mother, Liz, hadn't lived there long, but it was a really rough neighborhood and my son had gotten into some fights. At first, I thought it was cute. My son was a little version of me. He got angry and heated like I did. Victor Jr. was following in my footsteps. It wasn't until my son threatened to hit a teacher, that I finally broke. It turned out that at some point the teacher was the one that said he was going to hit Victor Jr. and my son reacted. This is when I lost my mind. I finally realized how following in my footsteps was destroying him. Of course, I got arrested again after I came home. That never stopped my love for my son and I would write to him and his mother regularly. I'd rarely get an answer, but it was still worth it. Victor Jr. was always in my heart, so hearing any information about him was worth it.

When I finally got out, I went to get some clothes from his mother's house. Victor Jr. was wearing my clothes and had the same expensive taste that I did. He was into really expensive sneakers and all that. I know he learned that from me. It didn't take long for me to realize that Victor Jr. was also into the same fast life that I was. It was my fault. All of it. I feel like I was finally changing, but I tried to act like the same person I always was. I was too ashamed as a father that I couldn't even sit down and talk to him. I was the reason he turned into a street hustler as I did, and I struggled but made excuses to condone it.

It took getting arrested with my son to finally make me change. We were selling drugs together. We got arrested as a team. Father and son. (More on that story in Chapter 25, The Benefits of Surrender) Even after all he went through, my son made it out. Victor Jr. doesn't sell drugs anymore and married a beautiful woman. In the end, I'm so proud that my son was able to overcome the life and standards I set for him.

PHASE 2: THE JOURNEY TO 1240

My anger and resentment quickly led to drug abuse and street hustling, because it was the only future I knew. I began using drugs at a young age, and it became a big factor in my life. I was stuck in a cycle, without the desire to leave. I had opportunities to change, but I wasn't ready. I accepted my choices, and the anger I felt led me to refuse changing my life. I plead guilty to anything they charged me with, and found that my choices and holding onto anger was an additional form of imprisonment, not much different than the cell I regularly found myself in.

CHAPTER 12

DRUG IS NOT A PROBLEM.
IT'S THE SYMPTOM OF A PROBLEM

I started using drugs when I was 13 years old. I was living with my father at the time, but would stay at my mother, Mami's, a lot. Frequently, I would visit Mami. So, most of my time was spent going back and forth from Manhattan to the Bronx to check on my mother and make sure she was alright. Using drugs began in junior high school and went through most of my adult years. Although I didn't like being an addict, the stress of being the man for Mami was a reaction to the anger and feelings of helplessness within me. I used to make all types of excuses and poor choices that led to many problems that followed.

I went to Junior High School 117. One day, my friend Nelson was headed out of class and I asked him where he was going. Nelson told me that he was going to get high, and asked if I wanted to go with him. I told him, "I don't really use that, but I'll go with you." We went to the pier off of 103rd Street and Franklin D. Roosevelt Drive. Nelson grabbed a bag of heroin out of his book bag and took a couple of sniffs. He pushed the bag towards me, offering me some. Nelson insisted even after I said no. "Just take a couple of sniffs, Victor. You are always so uptight. This will make you feel good." I felt like I had to be the man in the family all the time, which was stressful, and I just wanted to relax.

So, I took a couple of sniffs and Nelson was right. It was my first time. In fact, I threw up. And then I felt so relaxed, like I didn't have a care in the world. Although I did feel good for a while, shortly afterwards,

Nelson and walked to a pizzeria and I felt like I could barely stay up. I barely remember ordering a slice of pizza, but I do remember that I couldn't hold it down. It felt like I threw up every drop of liquid or ounce of food in my stomach.

The next day, Nelson found me at school. "Yo. I'm going to the pier; you want to go," he said more like a statement than a question. The feeling of throwing up instantly entered my head. "Nah, man," I told him, "that tore me up." He smiled and responded casually, "We're not going to sniff. We're going to shoot it, that way we'll know when to stop. We'll shoot it up slowly." Maybe I was already addicted, but I couldn't help but say, okay. It wasn't long before using heroine became a regular thing. Nelson and I started shooting up daily. Heroine then took control of my life.

When you're addicted and craving a drug, this is what we called, "getting sick." When I got sick I used to yawn, get stomach cramps, get sweaty, and I had diarrhea. One day I was sitting in class, yawning, and I started to feel uncomfortable. It felt like I had a fever and I couldn't sit still. Even while being in pain, I felt desperate for a fix so I could relax and feel good, just for a little.

That afternoon, Nelson invited me to the pier like normal, but this time I refused. "I don't feel well," I told him, only to hear Nelson laugh after. "Of course, you don't feel well. You have a habit. You've been doing this every day for like a month now." I didn't know how to respond, other than saying, "I ain't no dope fiend." Nelson laughed even harder this time. "Ok" he responded, and I instantly started running to the bathroom. There was pressure in my stomach, and I started to feel more pain than I ever had before. I barely made it to the toilet to throw up. Nelson followed, watching as I withered in pain. "Look, Vic, you have a habit and I'm going to prove it to you," he said. "Let's go down to the pier."

I was in pain, but I followed. When we got there, he started setting up. "I don't have much," he muttered, "but I have enough to give you a G shot to help with the pain." I was willing to try anything. He got straight first, then he gave me the G shot. A G shot is when you're getting high and with someone else and they give you a little of the leftover. It's a process to get the heroin in your bloodstream. When you get high, you need a metal cap (a wine bottle cap or a soda bottle cap), an eye dropper with a rubber band on top of the eye dropper to use as a suction, a cotton ball, a belt or rope, and a needle. I used to draw water (to half the dropper), put it in the cap, cover it with the heroin and put a low fire under it so the heroin would dissolve. Next, you need to put the cotton ball in there and put the needle on the tip of the eye dropper. The cotton ball acts as a filter, as you put the needle to the cotton and draw the heroin up. Next, you tie yourself up with a belt, and then shoot it into your vein. You'd know you got a hit because a little bit of blood would get drawn out first and then you'd squeeze the heroin into the bloodstream. The G shot is a smaller shot from the first hit. You leave a little in the spoon or bottle cap. This is what Nelson left me.

As soon as the heroin hit my vein, I could taste it in my mouth. All the pain vanished instantly. Everything evaporated. Nelson didn't give me enough to get high, but it was enough to take me off the "ill". After a few moments, I looked at him. Nelson smiled and said, "See what I told you." I was addicted because of the physical pain that I was going through.

Even though I was just in Junior High School, heroine was only the start of my drug addiction. I only snorted drugs one time, but I quickly started skin popping (injecting under the skin) and went straight to mainlining (into the bloodstream). I was strung out by the time I was 15. I was attending junior high at P.S. 117, and I cut classes more and more. I was a pretty smart kid, so cutting class didn't make a difference. Even though I cut math class regularly, I would still get 100's. Getting good grades didn't matter though. The principal and teachers wouldn't pass me because I missed so much class. One of my math teachers made a deal with the administration to bring this smart student and put him up against me in a math challenge. The teachers and principal made a deal: If I won, I got to graduate. That's how I graduated, then went to Benjamin Franklin High School.

My brothers' friends always checked on me and when I got to high school, they were able to check on me regularly. They were always on top of me making sure I wasn't doing anything wrong. My brother's friends had no idea of my drug habit, and by then, I had started selling. I wanted to be around the drug as much as possible, because I liked the feeling that heroin gave me. Nothing bothered me. I found people to help my habit, like the elder person in the neighborhood, name Levi who lived near us. I used to take advantage of Levi when he was "sick" by giving him money to get the drugs that he needed. We would get high together and Levi would tell me to quit. Who was Levi to tell me to stop? Besides, he didn't pay attention to how much I would take because he was too high, so I would take as much as I could. And he was just one of many.

It might sound odd to say you have control over a drug, but that's what it felt like at the time. I would justify my addiction by saying, "Heroin didn't have control over me when I shot up; I controlled it." Some people wanted just enough to feel good and stopped once they were there. That was me, I used enough to feel good. I wanted to get high to the sky, but not to get out of control. Unlike some people who were greedy wanted to go into space by getting high while they were already high. Even if they were already high, they would see you about to get high and say, "Let me get a taste." This made their addiction that much stronger, because they got used to higher potency. I justified my addiction because I didn't take another hit until I started feeling sick again and I would stop when I started feeling good. That was good enough for me.

My drug addiction came from stress and anger, like the pressure of being the man of the house for Mami and not wanting to disappoint her. I was reacting to anger from my father. Although I was addicted to heroin and other drugs, I made sure to hide it from my mother. Mami had suffered enough for me and to add extra burdens on her would have destroyed me. I had to be more for Mami. I just didn't want to hurt my mother any more than she had already suffered, but at the same time I needed to find a way to cope.

CHAPTER 13

CHOICES AND CONSEQUENCES:
FEEDING THE MONSTER

Hustling in the drug game was second nature. I only sold drugs to get high and make money. Selling was an easy choice because most of the guys I got high with sold as well. One told me, "Instead of trying to get money out there to get high, if you sell, you make your own money and will have enough to get high." It opened my eyes to all new opportunities. He gave me half a load, which was 15 bags, and I sold for $2.00 a bag. I would give him $20 of the earnings, and keep $10 for myself. I was easily able to supply my habit, so I started using more and more. Eventually, it caught up with me and I couldn't make enough money to take care of my habit. I started getting into a lot of stupidity, like shorting drug dealers and getting deeper into debt. They started to threaten me, but I didn't care. The only time I worried about anyone doing anything to me was when I was "sick." As long as I was high, I didn't care who confronted me. It's simple: When you are sick, you can't fight; but when you are high, you don't feel any pain.

In 1970, I was selling on 111th Street when a big riot started. The Young Lords gang were on 111th Street and Lexington Avenue and took over a church and the police had to control the area. During the riot, I was arrested for selling. It was the first time I got arrested for drugs. I had been arrested for other things at that point, but they were petty. Not this time though. They sent me to Rikers Island and I had to kick heroin cold turkey at the time. Kicking a habit is a very hard and very rough experience. Every day I felt like I was going to die. Without my heroin fix I started yawning, then I started getting cold sweats. I felt nauseous. I almost swallowed my tongue. The Correction Officers came in and took me to the infirmary. They gave me a shot of morphine to stretch out my nerves and relax my muscles. Right after that, I felt stable and stayed overnight for observation. I thought I was good and that I was going to stay there to finish detoxing, but the next morning they took me back to my dorm.

Not long after I returned to my dorm, I started kicking all over again. After so much yawning I actually caught lockjaw and because I was 17 years old, I was sent to ARS (Adolescent Remand Shelter) in Rikers Island. The next morning, they sent me to dorm 17. In dorm 17 there was a room full of cots and about 20 other guys in there kicking habits too. I thought I was done for, because I was in so much pain, I was cold and uncomfortable. I couldn't sleep on the cot because of my stomach pains. It was terrible. A nurse used to come in a couple of times a day to check on us but she could only give me aspirin. There was no medication back then to help you detox so they would just say, "You look better than yesterday," even when I knew it couldn't be true.

In dorm 17 we had beds and a shower. I was there for almost six months and was convinced I was going to do the right thing when I came home. But that's not what it is like when you are addicted. It takes maybe 3 days to physically get the drugs out of your system, but I've heard it said that it takes 3 years mentally. Even though I got physically clean in Rikers, I didn't stay that way for long.

When I was finally let out of Rikers, I went home and almost immediately started using again. I was so mentally focused on getting drugs that I was physically getting all the effects of withdrawing again. It got worse after my mother died. I started doing crazy things. Since she was gone, I didn't care. When I fought before, it was for revenge. After she died, it just became a part of who I was. I did foul stuff, like robbing drug dealers, stealing their stashes, and getting into fights just to hurt people. It escalated to the point where I jumped from borough to borough stealing a stash in Manhattan and then go live in the Bronx until everything quieted down. Then I'd do something in the Bronx and travel to Manhattan to lay low. Once, I even went to Brooklyn to stay with my aunt and avoid both places. I slept wherever I could feel safe.

I used daily to build up my habit and found myself back on 115th Street between Third and Lexington. Once again, I was selling. Every time I got a package, the first thing I did was get high and last thing I did before getting another package was get high. I sold drugs just to feed the monster, which led down a path of bad consequences.

CHAPTER 14

"JUST ONE MORE HIT!":
THE PRICE ADDICTS PAY

In the 70s, I was moving up as a seller. I no longer sold heroin; instead, I started selling weed and cocaine. I finally started making real money. Once my mother died, I didn't care where I was or living or who I hurt. I moved around to any place I could stay. My life moved fast living from placc to placc and moving up in the drug selling game. Money and drugs took over my life.

The moment I started selling cocaine, I stopped using heroin. Since I was selling cocaine, I almost always had some around. Smoking weed and sniffing cocaine became so normal, I would do it daily. I snorted so much cocaine it tore a hole inside my nose, from one side to the other. Snorting cocaine caused it to numb for a while. Each morning, when I would brush my teeth, chunks of blood and tissue would come out of my nose. My nostrils literally became raw.

While I was in a club one night and saw a guy I knew, Steve, that ran the streets in the drug game. Steve particularly dealt in heroin, but didn't like to get high. My nose was burning and crusted with scabs. I was desperate for more cocaine and of course, the pain would come again, which created a cycle. Not only would I shoot or snort for the high, but to also relieve the pain.

Steve, the drug runner said, "You look terrible, man. Terrible." I didn't realize it, but Steve came up to me with a concerned look on his face. I told him what was going on, how much pain I was in. "I know what would help you, but I don't want this for you," Steve whispered. I instantly knew what Steve was talking about, and smiled as he handed me a bag of dope. "If you sniff this," Steve said, "you are going to be good as far as pain."

I was a strong person, but my system was so out of pocket. Even though I had stopped using heroin, my system was still open to craving the drug. I thought I had control over it because when I relapsed, I could feel myself getting bent out of shape. It's why I would stop. And it felt like I could. But in reality, I couldn't. So, I sniffed that bag of dope, but not for the high. I was already high from the cocaine. I did it to take away the pain, and it took the pain away all day. I was good again, and again, and again. I added heroin back into my mixture of drugs, which continued to include cocaine and weed.

It was a struggle when I was down, from using drugs, and I lost a lot of friends during the process. A few of my friends turned their backs on me when I started getting high but others were really concerned for me and wanted me to stop. One told me, "I'll give you the world if you stop getting high. Just take this money and do what you're going to do. Don't ask me for no more money, though. This is it. You can ask me for whatever you need when you get clean, but you gotta stop first." But I was more interested in getting money to get high.

I ran out of product once and spoke to my connection, asking for more. The drug connection sent somebody to pick up the money and had me on hold. The connection kept telling me it would be a while or that they would get back to me, and the waiting caused me to get "sick." I was sick and desperate, so I bought a few bags then bumped into my brother. After my brother found out that I was getting high just like him we would often times get high together. Instead of going into the house to get high, I took Junior to the roof with me to shoot up. It was the first time I realized what real drug addicts were like. Junior and I were on the roof, and I had just put the heroine into an eyedropper after cooking it. I would take an eyedropper, fill it with water, and mix it with the heroin on the spoon to dilute it. The heroin would dissolve in the water. Then you would draw all of it back into the eyedropper, put the needle into the dropper, and use the needle to shoot it into your bloodstream. I was going through the routine when I was interrupted by some guy we were with asking me what water I used. I showed Junior the bottle, and he responded, "My bad, man, that's not water. That's my urine." I was so "sick" at that point, I didn't care. "I'm not throwing this away," I responded, hotly, "I ain't got no more money."

As I put the belt around my arm, I heard people running up the stairs, and right before I slid the needle in, I realized it was the police. "Drop everything you got," they yelled. "Arrest me if you want," I murmured and pushed the needle into my arm, squeezing the whole thing in. I didn't care. I didn't know who I was. Instead of being Victor, I was a heroin addict. Nothing stopped me. I was fully invested in the addiction. It owned me.

CHAPTER 15

OTHER ADDICTIONS

Getting involved with using drugs, often leads to other bad choices and addictions as well, and you react to feed those other habits. I spent a lot of time selling lots of different drugs, like weed and others. But when I only sold weed, I wasn't making as much and started gambling. At the time, I had fully stopped using heroin; and was only smoking and selling weed, which was like smoking cigarettes. Gambling was a completely different high. Sometimes I was broke for months because I would lose every day, and every now and then I would get a winning streak and have lots of money. Gambling taught me how to enjoy that money while I had it. But it wasn't enough to make me quit selling. I had to sell because I would waste money getting high off the product, and I had to make fast money to even out my addiction. If I spent $60 getting high, I had to sell enough to make that back.

Over on the corner of 115th and Lexington, near the grocery store, I was playing a dice game called Cee-Lo. Cee-Lo is a game with three dice. You throw the dice and if you hit 4, 5, 6 on the dice that's Silo. When you get two pairs and then another number you have to try to beat that number. The only thing that beats this is Cee-Lo or three of a kind. We played this game everywhere. People were just throwing money down on the ground and those were the bets. When you won, you collected all the money.

It was a really hot game, and I was on that day. No matter how I threw the dice, I won. A guy who I had never played against came up, asking to join. Joe was Nate's cousin, one of the guys I grew up with, so I had seen him around. Joe was a healthy guy, and I could tell he was really strong from the muscles that stood out from his dungarees and tank top. When he pulled the wad of cash from his pocket, I knew he was a drug dealer. That didn't bother me too much. With the way I was playing, I could win all of his money.

We started to play, and Joe couldn't win a bet. When he finally did, he doubled down only to lose it. I won easily, and it frustrated him. But Joe didn't stop. Joe kept placing bets until he was at the very last of his money. By now, he was angry. Joe started mumbling and cursing under his breath. He was tense. He started accusing me of cheating. I handed him the dice and told him to check it out, but that wasn't good enough for him. Joe leaned close to my face, his voice rising, with his head leaned back slightly as he arched his. As he was talking to me, he was spitting directly in my face. My hand instantly went to his chest, pushing him away from me. "Back up, man, you're spitting on me," I warned him. "You robbed me for my money," Joe said in between a mixture of cursing. Joe wanted to make sure there was no question to whether he had accidentally spit in my face, he then made sure it was known. Joe looked me square in the eye and let out a puff of air as his spit flew from his lips. In an instant, he started swinging. I was alert enough to know that the spit was a signal. I was ready and already lowered my body by the time he went to swing. I hurdled forward, grabbing Joe waist and swiping his feet, pushing him to the floor. Like a machine, I climbed on top of Joe and started hitting him. Within seconds, my friends surrounded and separated us.

Nate seemed frantic. "Yo, Vic, that's my cousin," Nate shouted, knowing me well enough to know the fight was far from over. "He swung at me. I didn't do nothing to him. He's saying I'm robbing him for his money. You know who I am. I got a right to be lucky one day. It's not like I win here every day. You know I play fair," I replied, heatedly. But Nate was Joe's cousin, so I was willing to end it. We scattered after that; Joe went his way and I went mine. I kept the money, even though Nate asked me to give it back. Another guy, someone who seemed to know Joe well, came up to me and said, "Be careful man. Joe smokes dust (pcp angel dust) and ain't wrapped too tight. He'll be back." I thanked him, which was my usual, and walked out. I stood out on that block for a while after that before I started to head home. I went into my building and went straight to my gun. I started carrying after that moment.

When I became addicted to something, it took a lot to change my attitude and my habit. Gambling was no different, and I returned the next day to start another game with the regulars. I knew to give my gun to Luke, one of my boys, because I didn't want to get busted for gambling and a gun charge. Luke was solid, so I knew I could trust him. I was still a little uneasy from yesterday's incident with Joe, so before I left I told Luke, "Hold this gun for me. Put it in the car. If you see something jump off, give me my gun." Just in case, I had a friend of my father's, Jackson, warn me if the cops were on the way. Jackson had known me since I was young and was always really protective. Jackson helped me multiple times in the past. His warning call was usually to yell, "Break it up!"

When something goes down, there is clarity in the chaos for those who regularly live it. I knew Jackson would say, "Break it up!" Normally lookouts say, "Bajando," (*going down*) to signal that the police are coming. This time was different. Instead of the normal "Break it up!" or "Bajando," Jackson screamed, "Victor!" loudly. That was the biggest red flag I could have gotten. My mind started racing, why would Jackson scream my name instead of using any of the signals? Why would Jackson call me, directly?

I had the dice in my hand ready to shoot, so I was already low to the ground. Instead of reacting and looking around, I tried to scope the area. I glanced between my legs and saw Joe with a shotgun barrel emerging from a bag and pointed in my direction. Joe heading right for us with a gun and he was looking for trouble. Suddenly, people started running. Joe was too far from me to jump or fight, so I grabbed the cash that was on the ground and started running. I knew not to run in a straight line when someone had a gun aimed at you, so I started darting from one side of the sidewalk to the next, zig zagging as fast as I could.

I heard the shot when I reached the middle of the block between 3rd and Lexington. I dove between two cars, trying to look back to see where he was at. I was barely able to see under the tire, but I could see the shotgun on the ground. I wasn't going to get another chance. So, I started running toward him. I knew if he had one shot ready, he would have more. And sure enough, I watched Joe reach down to pick it up again as I was running in his direction.

I instantly turned around to run away from Joe. I made a left on 115th and 3rd Avenue towards 116th and 3rd Avenue, which was usually a crowded area at the time. I figured he wouldn't shoot into a crowd, so I thought I would be safe. If I made it there, I could get away. I looked back to see him sprinting towards me, the shotgun swinging in his hand. It looked like he was headed to 1st Avenue.

I started to realize the chaos the shot caused. Everyone was running and there was a lot of commotion. I knew he would have a harder time getting to me because of the chaos. It was my chance. I could sneak away, but not without my gun. I needed it in case he found me; I needed to be protected. I headed back to my house and found my friend Luke, who was supposed to hold my gun. I grabbed my gun from his hands. "Why didn't you give me my gun?" I demanded. Luke said, "I didn't want you to go to jail." I almost laughed. "You didn't want me to go to jail?" I asked, looking straight at Luke. I repeated the words my mother told me since I was a baby, "I prefer to be in jail than dead." I was livid, "Joe tried to kill me!" I took the gun and left to find Joe.

I jumped into my car, my hands shaking while trying to get the key in the ignition because I knew I didn't have a lot of time. I instantly hit the gas, not looking, and heard the crunch of my bumper against the trunk of the car in front of me. I became enraged. I grabbed my gun, climbed out of the car, and slammed the door. I headed to 1st Avenue to find him. I knew the police were following me, but I didn't care. All I wanted to do was find Joe. However, Joe was lost in the mix. I searched for his face, his gun, but couldn't find him in the crowd.

When I got to 115th and Lexington, there was a beat cop waiting to talk to me. "You want to talk to me?" I asked nervously, "About what?" With a deep voice, he said "You got shot at? There was a thing here." I acted like it didn't matter, but the beat cop told me he saw me running. "You saw everyone running," I responded to the cop, and started to walk away. I had to get the gun back to the apartment. Something caught the cop's eye, and I managed to sneak away.

When I came back down from my apartment, the cop was still standing there. "I know he was shooting at you," the cop repeated. I didn't know what to do but act innocent, he couldn't prove I did anything. "I don't know what you talking about. There was shooting, everybody was running. I don't know what you mean," I faked ignorance, but the cop wasn't buying it. "I'm just going to say that if anything happens to him...," he said coldly, "I'm coming for you." Even with that threat, I knew that if I could find him again I would kill him.

Joe must not have felt safe, because within a few days his grandmother came to the Italians to talk about the situation. She must have known that my family, including myself, worked for them. Joe's grandmother begged them not to do anything to her grandson. Of course, this came back to me. My boss, Vance, called me into his office and said, "Victor, we heard of the situation that you had. I spoke to Joe's grandmother and I promised her that you won't do anything to him." I was furious. "You're asking me not to do anything to him after he took a shot at me to take my life? You could tell her that he took his chance, so I'm going to take mine. If I miss, I miss, and after that I'll let it go." Vance went silent for a second, looking at me intently. He saw the anger in my eyes, and waited for me to calm down. "You're misunderstanding me. I'm not asking you. I'm telling you. Let it go!"

I was furious. Who did he think he was? Vance couldn't control me like that. Vance let me blow off steam, then pulled me aside. "Listen," he said, "I understand how you feel. If it makes you feel any better, we told her that you were not going to do anything to him. But we also told her to tell him to stay away from you. If he doesn't, we will come in and take care of the situation."

That's how it stayed. I stopped hanging out on my block to cool things for a while and started hanging out on the West Side.

CHAPTER 16

THE DRUG GAME

I was constantly moving from place to place as an addict and a dealer. When I relapsed, I started hanging out downtown on 74th and Broadway. I was hiding down there because I owed some money to this guy and that guy. At one point I found a group to hang with on 112th Street, and I made a business out there between 2nd and 1st Avenue. I used to sell 1,000 bags of heroin a day at $10.00 a bag, so I was making good money. But I started to get paranoid. I felt like many people were trying to set me up to hurt me. Because I made money, people would tell me false information and gossip to see if I fell into their trap, or they would cause bad blood with different guys. They would be sneaky and find ways to set me up. For example, if I got robbed, several people would work together so I couldn't find out who really robbed me. So, whenever someone brought me information, I would usually say, "It's alright, I knew that" or "Thank you," and try to keep my eyes down, but I was open and aware of my surroundings. It didn't really matter who; at this point, it always felt like I owed somebody money or had to watch my back.

There was a hotel out there that everybody used to know called Milk Palace. Milk Palace was a big hotel with a lot of illegal activities. It had a huge carpeted lobby with rooms that weren't high class but very big. It was back in the 70's, so you can imagine the bright and loud colors. It was no Hilton and it was no Sandals Resort. Out of the traditional ghetto hotels of Manhattan, it was one of the better ones; cleaner. It got worse throughout the years but it was clean at that time. It was here I learned you are never the only one in the drug game. There is a person who owns the drugs and his bodyguards, a person who sells, the girls who look for the dream and did whatever it took to get money, and the girls who love the environment. So, the Milk Palace was the perfect place for everyone to be. It was filled with drug dealers, prostitutes, homosexuals, and drag queens. And it was always busy, so cops were there every day.

One evening, some random white guy came and asked if I knew any prostitutes. The majority of the men looking for prostitutes in that neighborhood were white during that time. The Milk Palace was a couple of blocks away from Needle Park (there's a movie made after this park called *Needle Park*). I was working the corner near Milk Palace, so when he asked me, I walked him right across the street. I wasn't doing this out of the kindness of my heart. The pimps paid me to do this. I was a runner and would use the money to get straight. So, I took him over to Milk Palace, and cops surrounded me. I was arrested for miscellaneous sexual something or other. I said I was guilty because that's what I did. Any time I got arrested, I would say, I was guilty and admitted to everything I had done or anything they wanted to charge me with that day. It was easy for me. Jail was like a vacation and I could rest. Also, I wanted to meet Junior's killer in prison and repay him for what he did to my brother.

My jail sentences never lasted long and I would be released only to continue doing the same things again. I went back to the Milk Palace because I paid for a room there. It was also quick money with the hustle for the pimps. I was hustling, but I wasn't using since I had to detox while in jail. I was kicking it and headed down the staircase to see a girl crying on the steps. Her name was Crystal. I asked Crystal what was wrong, and she started to break down. Crystal told me that she had a pimp and he would regularly hit and abuse her. My mind instantly flashed back to my childhood and my mother crying after getting hit. It bothered me, badly, and I could barely hold back my anger. "Why are you selling your body to give him the money?", I demanded. Crystal only uttered lame excuses, and I could tell it was just out of fear.

"You don't really want to do that for him no more," I said as a statement, not a question.

"No, but…," as Crystal's voice trailed off.

"Don't! Just tell me yes or no." I needed her answer, I said.

"No, I don't want to be with him," Crystal muttered between sobs, almost gasping.

"Okay, no problem," I pronounced.

I went to get a gun, and headed straight to where Crystal's pimp was usually located. The pimp was black. Almost all the pimps were black in my area at the time. He was outside sitting in his car. "Leave her alone, or you'll have to deal with me." Crystal's pimp could tell the seriousness in my eyes I walked straight towards him, cocked my gun, and pointed it to his chest." He didn't say a word. I only knew a few people in that hotel, and I'm sure he knew a lot more, but the pimp was shook and didn't bother her after that. The pimp must have been new to the game because he gave in too easily. Other pimps had a crew that would have taken me out.

When I saw Crystal next, I told her she didn't have anything to worry and that he wasn't going to hurt her. "Who are you?" she asked, blankly staring at my face. Within a day, three of her friends were in my room saying they didn't want to work for anybody either, but they felt comfortable giving me their money. The prostitutes said that giving it to a man made them feel well protected, and the girls started giving me their money here and there. For a short while, I took the prostitutes' money to support my habit, but never fell into the pimp game. It wasn't like me and didn't fit my personality. But I was getting money from these prostitutes regularly. They would bring stacks of money for me to hold for them. At the same time my drug habit continued, so I needed the extra money and I didn't really care.

Shortly afterwards I went to prison again. After spending some time in prison, I got out and the same girls found me again and wanted to give me all their money. "Nah, that ain't me. That ain't me," I told them. "You girls got to stop." I couldn't take their money anymore and wanted to move on. So, I left that neighborhood and headed back to 115th Street, where people knew and loved me. The problem was, they all loved me for different reasons. Some loved me for what I provided as a drug dealer, and others loved me enough to beg me to stop. It didn't matter though because I was back home.

If nothing else, it was my honesty that caused a lot of people in the game to trust me. They knew that if I was around them and I got arrested, I wasn't going to snitch. It was part of the game, and necessary if you wanted to stay alive. I never told on nobody in my life. Sometimes, I would say, "Man, I get busted for anything. But I'll do my time. People get busted with drugs on them, guns on them, and they don't ever do a day. I got bad luck." When I used to hustle, there was always at least one person around who had my back though, even when I didn't expect them to. I don't know how, but every time I got over my head into trouble, someone would come *save* me. When I was in trouble I had people that would fight with me. So, I didn't really have to fear. I gave all the credit to myself, though. I was the man. I felt that I was untouchable.

CHAPTER 17

FINANCES AND GIVING FREELY

Because people see new cars, clothes, jewelry, and excess money, they believe drug dealers have an easy or good life. That's far from the truth. Dealing is not a life, and it gets worse with each step deeper into the game. People have no idea what goes on behind closed doors with drug dealers. They don't see the many enemies who are ready to kill for what people in the game have. They don't see the endless nights and insomnia. They don't see the paranoia of looking for police at every moment. Sure, no one wants to work for a week only to get paid $450 and then have to pay $150 in taxes, $250 in bills, and only keep $50. All you can really do with that is relax on the couch. But you don't think about the fact that you don't have to worry about someone trying to stick you up or shoot you for that $50, on a daily basis. Plus, you get to spend it with people you want. Dealing doesn't give life, it only takes from you, that's why I say it's not actually a life at all.

I don't know if I ever even classified myself as a dealer, because I was a kind and giving person. I spent more money than I can count. If I would have saved all the money I made those years of selling drugs, I would probably have been a millionaire. But people were right when they said, "Vic, you spend money like you're a millionaire and you ain't got none." I never had excess money, I'd always spend it. It was hard not to. It almost made me feel like a normal person, instead of a drug dealer. I was just so involved in that life and it was the only way I knew to live the life I wanted. And that life was expensive. In addition to all the drugs and paying for protection, I went to nightclubs, regularly. I would stay in an after-hours club every day, going in about 7 – 8 at night and not leaving until 9 in the morning. I'd eat dinner when I woke up and breakfast to go to sleep. And I would eat when and what I wanted.

People would tell me I was just letting the money go by or that I never had any money. I would never have money because I was specific about where and who I sold to. Addicts would get mad at me when I didn't sell to them or have money to borrow. I would say, "I don't have none. I don't have none." That was only one reason why people called me a weird drug dealer. For example, I would never sell to a pregnant woman, even though I knew others who would. I even caught one of my guys selling to a pregnant woman, and I took his stash and told him he wouldn't hustle for me like that anymore. Watching what people would go through to get drugs, like having me hold onto their welfare card or check, broke me. I didn't want to stoop to that level. I liked making fast money, but not at that expense. I believed I had all I needed without doing that. I never wanted to be a millionaire or be considered rich; I just wanted to make enough money to support my habit.

I would never have been rich because I was so free with my money. As soon as I made it, I gave it away. I didn't want to be stingy. On 115th Street was where most of the alcoholics were, but many people liked to label them bums. I don't know, maybe they were just people with problems. Anyway, I would always go to the block and give them a few dollars. They usually took it to the liquor store on the block to get right. But I did it for a reason. I didn't like how people would judge and abuse them. I mean, really, no one is an angel, we all have some form of addiction. And I could spare a few dollars to help them.

My generosity paid off at times. When I was arrested in Rikers Island, a Correction Officer (C.O.) came up to me and said, "Victor Muniz, let's go." I asked a higher officer who ran the block where I was headed, but he said, "I don't know man, just go with him if he's picking you up." This wasn't normal, so I started asking questions like crazy.

"Where we going? Why are we going through here? Where are you taking me?" but he remained quiet. He just looked forward and made sure I followed him. We finally got to a dorm, and the C.O. quietly said, "Tell Willie 'I'm here.'" That was it. No explanation, no emotion. But I did what he said.

A guy came up to me with a bag of commissary, a chain, and a watch. I couldn't help but stare at him. "Who are you, dude?" I asked. His laughter filled the room, "You don't know me, man? I'm the guy you used to give $5 or $10 to every day to drink some wine." I still didn't recognize him. I used to do that often. "You run the streets," he laughed even harder, "but I run this joint in here. Whenever you need something, tell your C.O. to call me and send a list of what you need. I got you. Thanks for having my back, brother. I love you."

Giving freely with my money didn't just help me in jail on a regular basis, but when I got out as well. Some of the guys I used to help gave me warnings, like "Yo, Victor, don't stay here today. Leave, Leave. The police is in the Health Station." Because I helped them so much, they knew I lived right across from the health station. I sometimes think that If I would have kept that money, that I would've been rich. Instead, I kept getting high and gave it all back. In fact, I could have been a millionaire, and despite the time I spent in and out of prison, freely giving a few dollars here and there saved me countless years in jail.

CHAPTER 18

WOMEN AND THE GAME

I never had a problem getting girls to like me. I didn't mistreat the women and I was never abusive; I couldn't after watching what my mother went through. Because of my mother, I wasn't the type of man to hit, abuse, or mistreat a woman. Instead, I had an easy come, easy go motto. I was free, but it was because of my mother. Anytime I was around a woman, I'd remember her telling me "A man can be born out of a woman, but a woman can't be born out of a man. You treat a woman the way you expect me to be treated." And although I didn't focus on love, I tried to make sure I was respectful. My mom taught me that men can be strong, but women can be stronger because they can hold more pain than a man. I watched her hold on to too much pain, and I didn't want to cause any woman to feel the same as she did.

My First Love

My first love was a girl named Maria. I met Maria when I was about 15 years old. We used to go to JHS 117 together, and she was out of my league. Maria was beautiful, soft-spoken, and kind-hearted. She agreed to be my girlfriend, but it didn't take long for my conscience to take over. "What are you doing?" I'd ask myself, "This is a good girl." I kept messing around with Maria, but I knew she was different. Maria was above and beyond the girls I normally liked. I knew I should have let her go, but I couldn't. Maria was my first love. She felt perfect.

One Saturday, Maria asked me to go to her church, La Hermosa, with her, and I agreed. I promised to pick her up at her place, and I walked

Maria and her two sisters to their La Hermosa church. I was nervous to meet her parents, but by the time I got there the rest of her family had already left. The church wasn't too far, but I started to get more nervous with every step I took. This didn't feel like the right place for a guy like me, and when we got there I knew I couldn't go in. Uncomfortably, I told Maria, "I'll see you tomorrow in school. I didn't want to let you down, so I walked you to church, but I'll see you tomorrow." As I left, my mind reminded me that I also had to let Maria go. This situation confirmed what I knew but didn't want to admit, that I couldn't date someone who needed me in church with them. After all church was not the place for a guy like me.

I tried to act normal the next day at school, but Maria knew something was wrong. As I started walking her to her house on 112th Street, I stopped. I quickly gave her a hug and a kiss, then said, "I need to talk to you." Her dark eyes started to blur, and pools of tears rested at the bottom of her eyes. I could see Maria's jaw clench when I said it. "Listen, I really like you," I started, "You're a great girl, but I can't be with you no more." The tears started to fall from the corners of her eyelids. "How could you say you love me and that I'm a great girl, but you can't be with me anymore?" Maria's voice wasn't harsh, as I expected, but defeated. I'm not sure where I gathered the courage, but I felt I had to be honest: "I'm no good for you. You need somebody better than me, but I will always love you." I listened to her start to sob as I walked away.

Women Later in Life

I should have taken my experience with Maria as a hint of what would happen later in life with women as well. I was married in the early 70s to a friend I grew up with. We got an annulment quickly after, but stayed friends and remain friends to this day. I thought I was ready for marriage because I knew her, because I trusted her, but in reality, my addiction and work were more important. I cared for Maria, and we remained friends, but it changed my mentality. I started to become a loner and focus on business: selling drugs and getting high. It's not that I wasn't good with girls anymore; in fact, I messed with a lot of girls. I just didn't feel anything. The relationships were empty.

When I was in the drug game, I could pull girls my bosses couldn't. Once, one of my bosses, James, made a deal with me about this girl he was trying to get with for a long time but couldn't. James saw me talking to her, and pulled me aside after. "Victor, you wasting your time. If I can't, you can't. Forget it." I don't know why she wasn't interested in him, he had money, but she wanted me. To the point where she offered to rent a room for me to share with her. James saw us the next day and was in shock. I confirmed what James assumed, and he offered me a thousand dollars. "It's for your expenses yesterday," he laughed. James had assumed I had to spend insane amounts of money to bed her. Those were the types of people I dealt with daily. But I wasn't like that. Even though I was popular with women, the relationships were always short lived and meaningless.

I tried to focus on business (the hustle), but opportunities came up with women regularly. Many of these women were beautiful, but drugs did something devastating to them. They would transform from Dr. Jekyll to Mr. Hyde. Some of these girls would ask me for credit and would happily tell me that they would do whatever I asked them to in order to get it. It offended me, as if they expected I was that type of guy. I didn't want girls to do any sexual favors for drugs. I'd tell them I don't do that or hand them the drugs they were after, then tell them, "Get away from me. Take this, but don't consider it credit." Sometimes, I'd even try to joke with female addicts and tell them, "I made a deal with the bank. I don't give credit and they don't sell drugs."

In my mind, the situation was simple. Well, fairly simple. I didn't get too committed to any relationships with women and especially didn't mess with married women, except for one girl. Her husband, Hector, abused the friendship we had, and I had to take the fall. I was running from the police one night, and I dropped the drugs to try to get away. I started banging on Hector's door to let me in, and he closed and locked it. Hector knew my call, my knock, but he made sure I wouldn't get in. The cops ended up catching me, and I got arrested. Similar things happened regularly, and eventually, my temper was so strong that I wanted to hurt Hector. I wanted revenge so bad I could taste it.

I was finally fed up with Hector one day, and grabbed my father's gun to settle the issue. "What are you doing, Victor?" my father asked, and I told him the whole story. My father laughed in my face. "What are you, stupid? This guy is doing this to lots of people. Hector will get his. It's not your place to do anything to him." My father is a rebel of sorts, and he started to smile while talking to me. Then my father said, "If you want to get back at him, if you want to get even, go out with his wife. Hector's wife's been after you for a long time. She even speaks to me about it regularly. Hurt him that way." I took my father's advice and infiltrated their family to the point where Hector's son would run to me before he would run to his own father. And that was the only married woman I had been with (that I knew of). I hurt Hector on a deep level, but it didn't really matter. My father was right. Hector would "get his," because not too long after, Hector was killed in a drive by shooting.

CHAPTER 19

GOD REACHING OUT

As I mentioned earlier, I seemed to always have protection around me while I was in the game. People always say there is a guardian angel watching over you. If I had one, it would be my mother. After my mother died, I didn't really believe in angels, but there were lots of coincidences where I should have been injured or killed, but nothing would happen. When things got rough, I would be hard to find or able to talk myself out of situations. Eventually, it was just easier to say, "I have somebody looking out for me." If I did, I figured it would have to be my mother. I like to think that my mother didn't know about my life choices, but in reality, I'm pretty sure she did. My mother just never told me about the negatives; instead, she would always tell me that I was going to make it in life. I believe she was always with me while I was in the streets.

Although I believed there was a God, I wasn't religious, so the fact that I sold across the street from a church and school didn't bother me. During school hours and on Sundays, I wouldn't sell. This was my way of being respectful to the church and the kids. Any other time was free game. Even though I respected God and the pastors, I sold next to the church. But like I mentioned earlier I didn't sell on Sunday because it didn't feel right to sell when church was open. The church was led by a pastor named Pastor Andrew. I wasn't doing this with any expectations from pastor Andrew. Because they saw me a lot, I think he was less likely to call the cops on me because he knew my face. It worked out in my favor. After I got arrested once, the pastor of the church went to my father and told my father, "I heard Victor got arrested." My father confirmed it, and Pastor Andrew asked what he could do. "I'll do anything. You want to go to the precinct? We could bail him out," he suggested. My father declined and asked him not to worry about it, but Pastor Andrew persisted, "My kids got everything they need. House paid for. College. They got everything. I'm not going out of my way. It's something I would like to do." I believe that Pastor Andrew saw something in me. Maybe God told him to do this.

I had two businesses and worked in a number hole, so I was fine with money and had a friend bail me out. Back then the number hole was an illegal gamble business. People bet numbers based on the horse races. When there was a race, they would tally up the attendance and that's how people would win money. When I got home, my father told me that Pastor Andrew had come by. I asked what for, and my father told me "Pastor Andrew wanted to bail you out. He wanted to ask me. I told the pastor no because you were gonna be alright. I think you should tell him though." I was shocked, but my father was right, it was a nice offer. I didn't want to disrespect the pastor at all. "Okay, Papi. No problem." I told him and left to find Pastor Andrew.

I wasn't sure how I was going to thank Pastor Andrew since I assumed that he would tell me to let go of the game and refocus my life, but I knocked on his door anyway. Pastor Andrew's face lit up when he saw me and he engulfed me in a hug. All of the planned words I had escaped me, and I was shocked by what I had said next: "Pastor Andrew, I'm just going to be honest with you. Do I believe in God? Yes, I believe in God. Am I ready for God? No, I'm not. I just want to tell you thank you for wanting to bail me out, but I'm not ready to go to church. But I do thank you." I had expected disappointment and judgement based on what I had said. But that was not what I experienced. Instead, Pastor Andrew smiled warmly, "You're welcome. Whenever you're ready, let me know." I didn't really know how to respond to that and wished the Pastor well as I left. I was not ready to surrender or forgive, but for some reason despite all I had done, God seemed to be reaching out to me with warmth.

CHAPTER 20

LOSING FRIENDS IN THE GAME

"Friend" is used loosely when you are in the game. An acquaintance can be a friend. A co-worker can be a friend. In the game, anyone you do business with can be called your friend. In reality, there is no friendship. They are the same people you are making money with, but they are also the same people who want what you have. They want your power, your money, and sometimes even your wife. It's a different aspect to the normal world we live, and when you go to prison, its open game: the same guys who rolled with you are fighting to take your spot.

When I started selling drugs for myself, I had to do things I didn't want to, regardless of friendship. Everyone in the game, at least at some point, would have to betray their "friendships." One of my main workers, Flaco, was coming up short on money, so he tapped the bags. By tapped I mean that Flaco would take a little out of each bag and create another one, so it looked like he had more product to sell. Of course, his customers complained that the bags were smaller. Flaco was sharing the drugs with people he knew, including my father, to keep it a secret from me. But there was no secret. It was something he really couldn't hide because customers complained. I pulled Flaco aside and told him that I loved him, but he needed to stop doing what he was doing. "If you do what you're doing with me to any other drug dealer, you're going to get hurt," I warned Flaco.

Flaco was my friend, so I wanted to give him another chance. I sent Flaco to buy some weed for me. The weather was bad. There were storms the night before, and there must have been at least 8 inches of snow on most of the streets. We were at my father's house on 115th Street, and Flaco had to make it to 103rd street to buy drugs, so I sent another friend, Ray, with him to make sure they got the product.

After a few hours, only Ray came back. "Yo, what happened to my man? Wasn't he with you?" I asked, confused. "When we were getting close, Flaco jumped out of the car at 110th Street and said he would walk the rest of the way," Ray responded as if I should have known what was going on. That triggered me; my street mentality kicked in. Flaco had on sneakers and the ground was covered in snow. Plus, there was no reason for Flaco to get out of the car. I knew something wasn't right.

I went outside to head home and decided I'd follow their route. Flaco got off at 110th street, and I lived on 112th, so it wasn't far. When I got to my house, the door was wide open. I ran in to check the apartment, but no one was there. I had given Flaco the keys in the past to get a few things for me, so maybe he had made a copy. I headed back to my father's place to see if he had made it back. When I got there, Flaco was sitting on the couch with my father smoking weed. "Where you been at?" I asked. Flaco was clearly shaking, and not because of the cold. "Oh, somebody asked me to buy them a bag of weed so I was dropping it off," Flaco replied. He didn't look clean. "We gotta go to the house to pick something up," I told Flaco. He refused, saying that he had something to do, but I knew how to convince Flaco. I made sure he was watching when I went to my father's room, pulled up the mattress, and grabbed a gun. "Let's go," I said, walking out in front of him.

The second we got into the elevator, Flaco confirmed what I already knew: he had entered my apartment instead of buying the weed I asked. When Flaco walked to my door, he looked startled. "Victor, the door is open." I put my hand on the gun and responded, straightly, "The door is open." I had left it unlocked on purpose. Out of nowhere, Flaco jumped in front of me and pushed the door open, running into the room and rolling like an action hero. It was dramatically comical. If it wasn't for my anger, I would have laughed. "Have a seat," I sighed.

I pulled out the gun and cocked it. "Tell me the truth, bro," I said, glaring into his eyes. "What are you talking about, Victor?" I laughed under my breath. "You came to my house and you took some stuff." Flaco's eyes darted, "Nah, Victor, I would never do that to you. You're like my brother. You took care of me." Flaco was gaming me, trying to play with my emotions. "Tell me the truth. I don't want to hurt you; I just need to know the truth. I can't believe we are even having this conversation. I trusted you. Now, what did you take from me?"

Tears filled Flaco's eyes in an instant. "I'm sorry, man. My habit is bigger than what you think it is. I already owe you money and didn't know how to ask you for it. I'll make it up to you. I promise." Flaco sounded like he was begging. I didn't fully know how to respond in that moment. "Listen, man," I muttered, "I'm always going to love you like a brother. Why don't you get in a program and get your life together, because if anyone else entered my house like you did, there would have been a very different result. I would have easily hurt or killed them." I was drained. My mentality changed in that moment. Instead of giving jobs to people I trusted, I knew I was going to have to find workers I didn't know so if I had to do something to them, I wouldn't feel sorry about it.

"I'll be here for you," I told Flaco, patting his back, "and I'll look out for you. I don't want you helping me in my business anymore. Take care of yourself, because if you decide to sell for anyone else, you're going to have to watch yourself. Other dealers won't care for you like I do. The games and things you are doing to me will cost you your life." I hugged Flaco, and we talked for a while after.

Flaco and I stopped doing business together. I had to make that decision to protect myself and my product. Flaco and I stayed boys even without the business. A few years after that moment, one of my new guys told me, "That main man you had, they killed him." Apparently, Flaco was caught stealing from another dealer, so they shot him.

CHAPTER 21

THE ROAD TO 1240:
FIRST TIME IN PRISON

The first time I went to prison was to Rikers Island. My first time at Rikers Island, I didn't know what to expect, but I was scared to death. I got to Rikers for possession of drugs. I was 16, and saying I weighed 90 pounds was pushing it. I had welfare glasses that stood out like the bottom of thick coke bottles around my eyes. Everyone said I had a lot of heart, but I was scrawny. Everyone tells you that they abuse young guys and take their manhood and that people run in groups. But it was my first time in jail. I didn't know what to expect. The prisoners were segregated back then, "If you are from The Bronx, go over there. If you were from Spanish Harlem, over there." Everyone would be locked up according to this, but they used to come down for recreation and hang with their own. Being at Rikers opened my eyes to so much.

I had to stay at the court building until the bus came to pick us up, which was around dinner time. I was instantly sent to the mess hall with the group while the Correction Officers took our stuff to the dorms. In the 70's, the mess hall or cafeteria at Rikers Island used to be really open and everything was made of steel. The tray where you got your food, the plates, cups, utensils, etc. That's how you ate. Everyone would be looking at you when you got your food and would watch who you talked to. I quickly learned not to accept anything when other prisoners gave you something because they wanted something from you. The lessons happened quickly: if I wasn't personally learning, I was watching others.

The first thing I got to do was eat with the mess hall population. The smell and look of their rice and chili will stay with me forever. We had a choice of drink, bread, and dessert. I couldn't focus on that. Instead, I kept my head down and focused on the line, making sure nobody got around me. It was really crowded, and it seemed like everyone in front of me had been in jail for a while. They were huge, with muscles rippling underneath their jumpsuits. I watched as the trays filled up before me. It seemed like everyone was getting multiple scoops. Then, it came to mine. I felt like I could count the grains of rice and number of beans. I knew I was small, but this was ridiculous. "Yo, can I get more food?" I asked the guy serving me. "What you want to do for some more," the server replied. Everything in me froze. Time stood still for a moment as I remembered what everyone warned me about. I couldn't focus. So, I just reacted on instinct. Although the tray was heavy in my hands, without realizing it, I lifted it over my shoulder and slammed it into the guy's head. I don't know how much time passed, but when I looked down I noticed he was bleeding. A lot.

Suddenly, everyone in the mess hall was rushing towards me. I didn't know what to do but run. I kept running until I vaguely noticed someone I recognized out of the corner of my eye. It was my brother, Junior. He was in jail when I got there. Then I knew I had back up. I was ready to fight then.

People started looking up to me after I hit the cafeteria server with the tray. I became the guy not to mess with or the guy with a lot of heart. Not being labeled as a bad guy helped me survive. If you think you're bad, there's always somebody that is going to try you because they want to be badder than you are. At the same time, you couldn't be soft, because they will take advantage of you. Being myself was what worked for me, but the mess hall was always tense after that. It seemed like something a l w a y s jumped off there. I felt for a while like I was the man, but a lot of the guys told me that I was, "really lucky. Having a riot in the mess hall usually means the C.O.s beat you up and lock you down." They were right. I was really lucky the whole time I was there. Very few things happened to me.

Part of the reason that I had few bad experiences might have been where I stayed and who I knew. I went to the Adolescent Remand Center (ARC) building the night after the mess hall beating. That's what they called it back then, I think today they call it House Detention for Men (HDM). There were about four buildings that made up ARC. Before I went to court I was in the 3 Block, but they transferred me out to 5 Block. It was a big place. Each Block was a different building with over 600-700 inmates. Right when I walked in, I heard a lot of guys call out, "Yo, shorty" or "Come over here, shorty." One guy asked if I wanted some cigarettes, but I knew to tell him I didn't want anything. I didn't want to owe him. I found a group of people I knew, and I had to wait a bit but I was brought cookies and a bag full of stuff that I used to get by.

I was going to court one day and Block 7 was so out of control that the guards released tear gas. 7 Block was always in trouble because they were the revolutionary Block. This is where the Black Panthers, Young Lords, 5 Percenters, and Muslims organizations were all located. The rioting in 7 Block was so bad that the police had released tear gas earlier that morning. In fact, when I entered the jail from the reception area my eyes started to burn. I couldn't stop the tears. My nose even started to burn from the tear gas that engulfed the block from earlier that morning. And the smell lingered for a few days. This wasn't the only time I went to Rikers; I ended up going multiple times and made connections that helped with protection with people inside like Vive and Arnold.

In prison I met a guy, we called him Vive, while I was in 5 Block. He was a young Puerto Rican with Vive Tu Vida (*Live your Life)* tattooed on his back. He was just a little over 4 feet and barely knew any English, if at all. Vive was crazy and hated bullies. If Vive saw any Hispanic crying or upset, he would instantly ask what was wrong. I'm not sure if the answer mattered or not, he would just start fighting or stabbing the person who was pointed out. While I was there, Vive was sent to the box (isolation) for 6 months due to violence, and that was the way he lived. We weren't really close, but Vive always showed me a lot of love, concern, and respect. It made me feel strong to know Vive had my back.

At Rikers, someone would get cut, stabbed, punched in the face, or beat up on a regular basis. The prison had to start making everything plastic because of how brutal people would be. Specifically, I remember a story about the mop wrings that used to be made of metal. One of my friends, Arnold, was the captain of the House Gang. These are the people that clean the block. The House Gang members had the privilege of staying outside while everyone else had to stay in their cells. They were the porters, housekeeping, etc. Arnold's build reminded me of Arnold Schwarzenegger, and it was just naturally how he was. Arnold didn't regularly go to the gym, but he easily looked like he did.

During the recreational hour in the block, which was called Lock Out, I had a little misunderstanding with a guy, and Arnold noticed right away. There were some threats, but nothing serious until someone snuck up behind Arnold and hit him in the head with one of the mop wrings. The mop wrings where thick and heavy and this would have knocked most guys out, but Arnold was solid. It just made him angry. Arnold turned around, grabbed this guy's shirt and pants, and started banging him against the brick wall. The guy started gushing blood. Arnold had the leeway to do certain things, and nothing serious happened to him.

There were riots that broke out during the incident, and cops came around to do investigations, but no one talked. The cops didn't get any information and that's how it was at Rikers. It might sound cliché, but the movies had it right. The depictions of people constantly fighting and acting territorial in prison was what I experienced at Rikers Island.

CHAPTER 22

OUT IN THE WORLD

No matter what jail I was in, it always felt like another world. When inmates talked about their homes, it was never a city or a specific place. They would always say, "out in *theworld...*" But that's what it felt like. Living in jail required you to live differently than you did normally "in the world". There is nothing you can control anymore. I was never out of prison for long. I would come and go regularly like a revolving door. I was in Rikers, Adirondack, Gouverneur and Clinton Dannemora. I even went to Watertown, Cape Vincent and went to Reception at Fishkill, which I do not discuss here. While in prison, I had to learn quickly that I shouldn't worry about what was out there and only focus on being inside.

Prison Gang Life

Out in the world where I grew up, there was a short era where people didn't believe there were any gangs in jail. In reality, the divisions were racial. People stuck with their races, blacks hung out with blacks and so on. And even then, there were differences within the groups. Not everyone in a group hung out together. There were regional divides as well. Brooklyn with Brooklyn, Manhattan with Manhattan. Well, Bronx was with Manhattan and Queens with Brooklyn, but that was the way it was. Either way, you always hung with your own group.

Although out in the world people didn't really believe in gangs, the gang activity was growing in jail in the 90s. Prison was full of Kings, Netas, 5 percenters, Muslims, Crips, Bloods, and even though there were tons of groups there was a lot of peace that way. Everyone liked being segregated, which meant there were no big fights. If one guy disrespected another, they would let them fight it out without making war. The inmates had the mentality that, "After this fight was over with, whoever won, won. There ain't no more fighting. That's it. If you try to get revenge, then it became like a little war between families."

Rikers Island (Institutionalized)

When I got arrested in '87, I was sent to Rikers Island and this time it wasn't my first time around. I copped out immediately and took the sentence. "I'll take 2-4 years," I said that because I thought ARS was bad at the time. They sent me to the 4 Building Block, where the minors were. I was in 3 Lower, and it was crazy in there. I went to the library and saw a guy with cops running behind him. He had two pencils stuck inside his neck, one on each side and the guys were screaming, "Look at Frankenstein!" In 4 Building Block, everyone had their faces cut and they took each other's stuff regularly, but nothing ever happened to me.

Before I got home, my parole officer used to call us in jail, even if we didn't get in trouble. She used to call us "institutionalized," which terrified me because I used to think that the guys in Rikers Island were institutionalized. Those guys didn't even think about going home, and most had 7 ½ to 15 years. Maybe she was right. When I got caught, I didn't care if I went to jail. I used to plead guilty even if I wasn't because I had an ulterior motive. I wanted to avenge my brother by killing the person who murdered him. Maybe this type of thinking did make me institutionalized. Even though I was obsessed to take revenge on his killer, it never happened.

Adirondack Prison

I went upstate NY for the first time in 1988 to Adirondack. While I was in Adirondack, it snowed that summer. It was another world. It was so close to Canada and freezing cold. I didn't realize that I had friends there until I heard, "Victor. Victor, Victor, Victor!" When I turned around, there were a group of guys that I grew up with and spent time in prison with. I was overwhelmed with love, and couldn't help but show them love when they approached me. They made being in jail easy. While I thank them, I can't help but think they were part of the reason I felt so comfortable going back to jail. When I was in prison with them they would get me clothes, like sweat suits, cigarettes, food, almost anything I wanted. Even when I didn't expect it, there were stoves for me to cook. I had been cooking since age 8, so I always found a way to cook it up and live it up with those guys while I was in jail.

While it wasn't abusive like Rikers Island, the inmates upstate in Adirondack found aggressive ways to settle fights. Inmates would say, "Let's do this like Puerto Rico!" and have dagger fights by tying their arms to each other, so the fighters couldn't run. When there was a conflict between two inmates, they used to tie their left hands together while each one had a dagger and they would go at it. Once one guy got stabbed other inmates jumped in to stop it. The inmates then took care of the guy who was stabbed by bandaging him up so he didn't go to the medical area and get everyone in trouble.

You get a work assignment in jail to make money, which most people used to get necessities such as food, toiletries, etc.. I made $0.45 an hour, which meant I made around $9 every two weeks. Doing well on my work assignment led to other opportunities. Besides my first job, I found myself as a bilingual teacher's aide as well. Then I ended up making $15.50 every two weeks. The inmates appreciated my cooking and because they loved my cooking so much, everyone told me, "don't buy food, just cook." Since I was a cook, I didn't have to spend money on buying food. Even my boys that I worked with told me, "just cook, don't clean dishes, don't do anything else. Take your food off the top and we'll take care of the rest." This advantage saved me from going to chow (meal time) and from using the little bit of money I made to buy food to cook.

So, I was able to spend all my money on coffee and cigarettes.

It was in upstate in Adirondack and Gouverneur where I started to get my life together. I was locked up in a dorm there, and the violence was particularly low, except in the gym. There were always fights in the gym, and I knew I had to remove myself from there. Even if I decided to work out, I thought to myself, "most guys would lose all the muscle when they got back home". It would be like turning from Popeye to Olive Oyl. Your priority would shift from working out to smoking crack or getting high. I was a small guy, getting big wasn't really a possibility, so I got my GED, worked through certificates and even started college courses while I was locked up. I needed something that would last longer than muscles, so I got my education.

The Riot in Gouverneur

While I was working on getting a college degree in Gouverneur prison, a riot jumped off near my dorm. All of a sudden, I heard an uproar, loud screaming. I got up to look and saw guys running to barricade the doors with mattresses and bunks to keep the C.O.s from coming in. The jail was shut down at the time. We sat all night in protest. Everything was quiet until the next morning, the C.O. said, "Get ready for chow." And we said, "We're not going to chow!" I knew the protest was planned because the inmates had provisions for us to eat, coffee, cakes, and other snacks and we were able to cook out of hot pots. We had food and could sustain for a while.

The riot started because the inmates felt they were being mistreated by the C.O.s. In jail, the majority of the population was 80-90% black or Puerto Rican, with a few Caucasians, and a couple of Dominicans, who wouldn't claim it. The Dominicans always said they were Puerto Rican to avoid getting jumped. Because the majority of the C.O.s were white, there was a lot of racial tension between the C.O.s and the inmates.

Then the C.O.s asked what we wanted.

The C.O.s tried to negotiate with the inmates and that's where I stepped in. There was a phone in the dorm to contact the C.O.. Since I was bilingual, the C.O. and the inmates chose me to be the spokesperson for our dorm. There was a lot of talking and negotiating. The C.O.s threatened to bring in Orange Crush. Orange Crush was almost like the National Guards of prison and they specialized in riots. When they are called to come in, it's the last resort because they take over the jail. Orange Crush had all the say and power. Even the C.O.s have to get out of their way. We could see them setting up out of our windows. Inmates started putting books under their shirts and tying them up so that if or when they got hit, it wouldn't hurt as much. They started putting wet towels around their heads in preparation for the tear gas.

The final negotiation was to have a sit-down or Orange Crush was coming in. The prisoners agreed to the sit-down. After the sit-down word was passed around to go to chow. We went to chow but it was straight to chow and back to the dorm. On the way back to the dorms the cops started singling people out and shipping inmates out to other jails. The cops were singling out who they thought was involved in the organization of the riot. Although I was a spokesperson, not an organizer, I ended up being singled out and was moved to Clinton Dannemora. The worst part about the protest is how it affected my college degree. When I was transferred to Clinton because of the riot, I lost all of my sponsorships and scholarships. The state paid for these benefits and once I was moved they were all forfeited. I couldn't get them back and couldn't complete my degree that could have helped me out in the real world.

CHAPTER 23

CLINTON DANNEMORA

Clinton Dannemora was another experience. It's impossible to really describe it. To me, it was the mother of all jails. Guys were doing life there, they had nothing to live for, and you could sense it just by walking in the room. At least, I could. I walked in with two other guys, and right away I could tell it was a prejudiced jail. The two guys with me were black and running their mouths, but the C.O.s were deathly silent.

We got to the front of the prison, and right in front of me was an unclimbable wall with an enormous, steel door going up to the C.O.'s lookout. I turned around and said to the guys with me, "They let you go with a lot of nastiness back there, but I'm going to give you some advice. You're really going into a different world now. Keep your mouths shut!"

Within minutes, we were shackled and lead to get our own bags. I had two heavy bags, filled with my college books. They took us back to the steel door, and two C.O.s came out. One of them was massive, both in height and muscle. He stood right in front of me, and I barely stood to his stomach. "You're in our house now," the other said, coldly. I could tell in his undertone that he thought we started the riots. "Let me tell you the rules of this house. Don't take drugs on credit because if you don't pay, they'll kill you. Don't look for fights or pick on anybody, because they'll kill you." I couldn't help but notice the repetition of "they'll kill you." It sounded like the inmates were the ones policing the jail. The massive guy added, "There's only two ways to get out this jail. You either max out or go home in a body bag." I was so speechless; I couldn't have gathered enough words to speak if I wanted. The stench of urine hit my nose, and I looked down to see a small pool near my feet.

One of the guys next to me who had been running his mouth peed himself. He was going to need a lot more advice if he was going to make it. The massive C.O. squinted his eyes, glaring at him in disgust. "You pissed on my floor?" he said, almost in a statement of shock rather than a question. "My cats walk through here and they go home with me every night. They're going to be dragging your piss into my house!" I didn't have the guts to look at the guy next to me as they called for a porter. Porters are the ones that clean the jails.

The porter arrived with a bucket and a mop, bigger than I had ever seen before. It must have been at least 30 pounds. The massive C.O. grabbed the mop from the janitor's hands and shoved it at the guy standing next to me. I tried to look down or forward, not watching him, but I could hear his sobs. Then I heard the guy next to him start sniffling, like he was crying as well. I listened as his shackles scraped the ground as he tried to mop up every drop, bawling. After a few minutes of trying not to react, the massive C.O. called my name. I looked up and met his stare directly. He held my paperwork in front of his face and smirked. "Pop, you're going to be alright here. In this jail, your people, the Macheteros, are here." Macheteros is a term used to describe an organization within the prison system. Some would refer to them as a gang. They were the original Netas. Macheteros are very influential in jail. I tried not to act in response. I just stood quietly. "You two niggers," he blurted, staring at the other two, "on the other hand, you better watch yourselves. They'll kill you!" If it was one of their tactics, it worked well. I was terrified for myself and them.

After all that, we were finally about to enter into the actual jail. It was old and musky, almost like a dungeon, with a long hallway. I watched the porters clean and noticed that my bags were starting to get heavy. I didn't want to look weak in front of the C.O.s, but they clearly noticed. "Make sure those bags don't touch the floor, because these guys work hard on them. If you mess them up, they're going to do whatever they want and I'm not going to get involved." It sounded like it should have been meant for just me, but I could tell the C.O. meant it to all three of us. I kept walking, trying not to let the bags sag at all, but the hallway was endless. My arms started to give out, but I said nothing. For some reason, the C.O. was looking out for me and called one of the porters to help. He looked at the other two and said, "You better not let your bags touch that floor."

They took me all the way to B Block then up to 6 tier. I didn't expect to have my own cell, but that's exactly what I got. When I walked in, I could hear all the inmates whispering about me. One guy said loud enough, "I'll see you when I lock out." I tried to stay calm and show no emotion. I don't know where I got the courage from, but I didn't falter. Recreation was called out, right after I got to my cell. I had been in the game long enough that I knew if I looked, I could probably find someone I knew. It wasn't long before I found someone I knew from the outside. The other two guys I came in with, though, I never saw them again.

The shower situation is one of the things I remember most about Clinton, because most inmates barely got that luxury. Most guys took showers Monday, Wednesday, and Friday, depending on the unit and if their block had enough showers. There were always showers in the gym, but those were rarely used. In the gym, they had open showers and you would be with everyone. You had five minutes. The whistle would blow at 4 minutes. You would go in and get wet, then have to leave when the whistle was blown so the next set of guys could go in. You'd soap up while you were out, then switch again for a minute. After five minutes exactly, the water would shut off. If you weren't clean, that was your fault.

I worked in the mess hall and was lucky enough to dorm with some guys that worked in the barbershop and gym, so we got to take showers regularly. Quickly, I started to feel at home again.

CHAPTER 24

OTHER SIDES OF PRISON

Although there were many difficult experiences in prison, there were valuable lessons learned. Sometimes, when you are in jail for a length of time, the inmates around you become closer friends than the guys you've grown up with. You don't have a choice; you are with them 24/7. It's not like on the outside where you see someone for a few hours and get to say bye. You live with these guys, and it's more intense if you are in a two-person cell. One of you will be reading in bed while the other is using the bathroom, and there is no wall to separate you. All of your cellees take showers at the same time you do because you have to go with your block. A cellee is a person who is in the cell with you. You end up doing everything with them, so it's impossible not to form relationships.

Changing Your Life

There are all kinds of people in prison. Most would go in and out, but a few would wind up changing their lives in there. Many times I would talk with some of the guys about how easily jail could become a revolving door, especially if you aren't afraid. Once you aren't afraid of something, it's easy to repeat. I remember always hearing, "He had to go to jail to become a Christian" or "He had to go to jail to change his life." In reality though, what difference does it make where you change your life? As long as it has changed for the better, that should be what matters.

When I was arrested in '96, I met an inmate from the Bronx. His name was Alex and he knew a lot about changing his life. Alex told me that he liked the way I carried myself. Which is funny because I played a character when I went to jail. You can't associate freely with everyone the moment you get into jail, so you create a persona. You find a way to appear defensive. I called it putting on a protective face. Alex and I started talking and found out that we knew the same people but had never met outside of the prison walls. Alex even knew some of my cousins, so it was easy to connect to him. It is odd how you practically make new family members behind bars.

Alex and I became so tight that he told me everything, like what had happened in the past or intimate details with his girlfriend. Even though I told him I wasn't into that, Alex would always share. At the time, there was a special girl named Myriam who wrote to me regularly. I always called her my best friend because there were never any signs of becoming a couple. He would always laugh and say, "This friend of yours, she's going to become your wife. I'm telling you." (More on that story in Chapter 27, Fully Surrendering).

But it wasn't just his personal life that Alex shared; he would even share stuff from his commissary without charging me interest. Normally, this wouldn't even be thought about. People have gotten killed for taking others food or supplies, but that wasn't how it was between us. We had a true friendship, where I could just go to his locker and get coffee if I needed some. And I made sure he could do the same. I learned a lot about how to become a true friend in prison, as unbelievable as it sounds.

Pride in My Work

I didn't just learn how to deal with others; I learned how to take care of myself as well. I met a lot of educated people in jail. One that really stood out was a doctor named Dr. Steve. He had a different mentality of why he kept going to jail. Dr. Steve helped to inspire me to realize that I needed to have a different mentality than most of the guys who wanted to exercise and look good. I needed to become educated so I could find a different life. A better life. So, while I was in Gouverneur, I decided to continue my education. I finished my GED and took some college classes. Although I didn't finish my degree, it opened my eyes. I was able to learn a little bit of everything through studying.

I decided to learn lawns and grounds one day while I was locked up. I don't remember what motivated me, because I grew up in Manhattan, Spanish Harlem. There was no grass for me to cut anywhere close and I thought I was always going to live in an apartment. But, for some reason, it intrigued me. And I found I liked it. Going out and cutting the grass was soothing. Before jail, the main animals I would see was a cat or dog. After lawns and grounds, I decided to work on the farm. I learned how to milk cows, clean gutters, and take care of livestock. From doing this I know that I could work on a farm and I really like it.

And I started to really take pride in my work. Regardless of what it was, I wanted to be the best at it. The best gutter cleaner was going to be me. Best groundsman? Me. Best farmer? Me. I treated the cows better than I would any of my pets. I'd feel guilty separating the newborn calves from their mothers or seeing which ones were destined to become meat. And these were just a few of the qualities that I learned in jail that I didn't learn growing up in Spanish Harlem.

I also learned how to become an actual survivor. When you're out dealing drugs and making money, the only people you have to get along with are the people making money with you. Otherwise, you don't really have to deal with anyone else. Sure, you work with others through a business lens, but you don't have to build a relationship with them. Buyers were dealt with strictly as business. When you're in the streets, your mentality is just about how you're going to make more money.

Life Lessons From Prison

Jail teaches you how to think differently. There is too much quiet time in jail, so it's hard not to just spend your free time contemplating other possibilities. I'd bet that most people, at least over 85% of them, stress while in jail. The other 15% learn to adapt and survive. And at times, in order to survive, you had to learn to turn your mind off. It might sound cold, but I couldn't worry or talk about what was going on outside those walls. I had to make them two different worlds. In my mind, it had to be, "you can't do anything about life outside of here, so why talk about it?"

Plotting life after jail became a downfall for a lot of inmates as well. There are so many people who make a master plan of how to get back into the street game without getting arrested. I couldn't help but laugh at guys like that. I'd listen to them say, "you know when I get out now, I'm not gonna sell drugs. I know these couple of young guys. They are loyal. They ain't snitches. I'm going to give it to them." I kept thinking, you are just going to give it to them and act like you're not in the game anymore? You giving it to somebody to sell. You're still selling drugs. I'd just chuckle and tell them, "the same way you thinking about not getting caught, the cops also thinking of how to catch people that's behind the scenes."

I became more of a friend, got educated, took care of myself, learned to survive, and changed my mindset while I was in jail. But more than anything else, I learned that everybody's rock bottom is different. Everyone has a different mindset or circumstances that keeps them down all the way to their lowest points of hopelessness. For me, my addiction and lowest points started with anger and stress from my father abusing my mother, that turned to drugs, street hustling and other poor choices that had negative consequences. Realizing that everyone has their unique set of problems and low points was one of the best life lessons I could have ever experienced.

PHASE 3: CHANGING MY LEGACY

Prison taught me more about myself and my potential than I can describe. I didn't realize how much my anger and resentment captivated me and held me down until I started learning more about God and trusting others in my life. Even when it appears hopeless, there is a way out. I was able to get out of the game, but that didn't mean that everything was perfect. I had financial and health issues that put all of my progress into question. In this phase, I learned what forgiveness really means and the impact it can have not only on those around you, but on yourself as well. By surrendering to God, I finally found true freedom.

CHAPTER 25

A REAL CHANGE

I finally started thinking about changing my life in the early part of 1996. I was at my mom's house, and I'm not sure what sparked the decision, but I knew it had to happen. I just didn't know when. I said I was going to change before, but I never took myself seriously. It was just to please others. This time, I felt it, hard. One day I was talking jibberish to my son, and realized that I was exhausted mentally, physically, and emotionally. I was just tired of everything I had been doing my entire life. Suddenly, while my son and I were chatting, a young woman walked in. I had known her my whole life, and it hit me. Without realizing it, I blurted out, "If I am ever going to change my life, I would like for her to be my wife." I don't know where that came from because I had never looked at her in that way before. She was simply a family friend. But at that moment, I could feel that she was a good woman, and I needed to change my life so I could be with her. Her name was Myriam.

You would think that was the movie moment – the exact second when I decided to become a better man. But it wasn't. I didn't give it much thought after that day. I went back to my norm: seeing the same old friends, doing the same drugs, living the life I knew. In fact, I started hanging out on the West Side again. I tried to keep it quiet, but I was fully in the game again. I started buying clothing and jewelry again, but there was a different feeling. I would look in my son's eyes and feel weight added to my heart. I felt so guilty that I couldn't be an example for him. But I couldn't focus on that. I had to let that go. I needed to make sure that moment passed so I could get back to the hustle.

So, I continued the hustle and decided to try and get a 9am-5pm at the same time. I tried to make money legally, but I was in and out of jobs. I wanted to be a good guy and also be out on the street at the same time, but it was impossible. One day, I was coming home from my legal job. It was November and slightly chilly, so I tried to hurry. When I got there, I saw cops arresting my son. Victor Jr. was laying down on top of a car, and the cops were hitting him. "Excuse me sir," I told the police officer, trying to be polite although I'm not sure my voice carried it well, "don't mistreat him. Arrest him if you gotta arrest him, but don't hit him." The officer looked at me, so I knew that I had his attention. He didn't move his anger to me, so it seemed like my tone worked. I repeated, pleading, "Excuse me sir, don't mistreat him. Just arrest him if he did something wrong." The officer grumbled in response, "Shut the f*** up and mind your own business."

"It is my business! That's Victor Muniz, Jr. and I'm Victor Muniz, Sr.," I told the officer. "Put your hands up against the wall," he screamed, pushing me, "We were told this was a father and son team out here." I was shocked that my actions caused this. "No, Sir! No! He doesn't have anything to do with this," I claimed, but they arrested us anyway. Both of us. Victor Jr. was a minor at the time. My son was in the game with me and because of me. We were selling drugs together. But he was only following my footsteps. My heart broke. I had never felt that kind of pain. Jail meant nothing to me. It was the fact that I set the example, I lead my son to this. And that I literally went to jail with him as a result.

That Fall of 1996, I was escorted into the bullpen at the Manhattan Courthouse, better known as the Tombs, where the C.O. let me meet with my son who was also waiting to see the judge. I had been in and out of the system enough that I knew a lot of the C.O.'s, so they granted me this opportunity since my son was underage, I was his father, and we were separated. They never let minors and adults stay together, so I knew it was useless to ask. The C.O. brought my son into the bullpen, and I grabbed him to hug him. "Listen, I'm sorry for what I have shown you to do in your life. You've followed my steps," I said, feeling the tears fall from my cheeks. Feeling that I had brought my son here. With great regret, many thoughts ran through my mind. I remember thinking, "Look where you're at Victor and you got your son with you."

The district attorney was offering me life this time. I had more than two felonies, so they were trying me as a career criminal. The legal aid assigned to me said, "I could get you a cop out, maybe 20 years to life or 7 ½ to 15 years." I couldn't imagine that. "Look, Sir, I didn't kill nobody. I'm not gonna cop out to none of that." The legal aid sighed and said, "It's election time, and they are hitting hard." The presidential election was in full swing, and promises were being made. If you were going to court for anything during this time, the law was being laid down and sentences were strict. The candidates wanted to let the voters know they were going to keep their word and keep crime off the streets. "Listen," I told the legal aid, "I don't care about no election. Really? I didn't do nothing to get no kind of life. Get my lawyer!" I knew what was going on, and I had to do something fast.

When my lawyer came in I told him, "Tell the DA right now that I will plead guilty to 3-6 years, at this very moment, under one condition: you let my son go." He looked around the room and then said, "Well... I don't think we can because-" I interrupted. "Sir, why can't you just do what I'm asking you to do and let me worry about the rest." My lawyer looked uneasy. "We'll see," the lawyer said, as he left the room.

I went to the bullpen again to talk to my son. "I'm sorry," I didn't know if I could find the words to fully apologize. "This isn't the life for you. For us. I'm sorry that you learned it from me. I'm going to cop out with the condition they let you go. I want to give you your life back. What I'm asking you for is if they give it to me, go home. Do the right thing and follow my steps when I come home, because I'm going to show you how to be better. Just as you followed my bad steps, I want to teach you the right way. I love you." I felt hurt. My heart was aching. I was ashamed of myself that everybody said I was a good father but I didn't go about it the right way.

My breath escaped my lungs when they offered me the cop out I wanted. I went in front of the judge while he described the charges against me in detail. With each one, I responded, "Yes, it was mine." As agreed, they let my son go and I was sentenced to 3-6 years. With the time I owed from cases before, it wound up being closer to 3 -11 years. Then they told me I was headed back upstate.

When I got in my holding cell, I leaned my head against the cold wall. I just said I wanted to change my life and I was right back here. "You need to stop," a voice said. "Think and do the right thing. You could do it." I didn't see anyone around me. I assumed it was my conscience and prepared my mind to head back to jail, back upstate.

The Change

The combination of my son going to prison with me, my exhaustion and motivation to move on with my life finally inspired me to do the right thing. At least, what I thought was the right thing at the time. I watched what I did and said while I was upstate to make sure I wouldn't trip up. I became a peer counselor. I worked with pre- and post-HIV counseling cases. I taught classes. I did everything I could to keep my word to my son, except go to church. I felt like it was going to be too repetitive, and I always made empty promises to God when I went to jail. Church just didn't seem like the right place for me.

While I was in jail, the young lady, Myriam, that I saw in Mom's house years ago asked Mom, "Hey, do you think I could write to Victor?" Mom said sure, so Myriam started writing to me. She was so positive. Myriam didn't write anything about getting together; instead, she was friendly and spoke about God. Very few women treated me this way, so it was hard not to pay attention and listen to her. So, I did.

Myriam started writing to me regularly. I used to go to jail like it was a revolving door, but this was the first time that a friend (someone I never did anything for and didn't have any pleasure of spending my money) focused on me. Myriam's kind heart had decided to write me, and I felt a gratefulness that I hadn't before. It meant more to me than I could describe and I started to cherish those letters.

Myriam would constantly write about God, and my heart started to believe what she had said. She showed me an honest love that reminded me of Mom. Myriam and Mom both sent me cakes and wrote to me regularly. It was the first time I got packages in jail. I didn't think life could get better, and I felt like if this continued I could stay in jail for longer. But I was finally torn because the people out there wanted me to love myself. They wanted better for me. I started writing back, and my head started to spin. I remembered the day when I saw Myriam, when I wanted to change my life to make her my wife. I had a reason to get back out in the world and I couldn't wait to get out.

I met with the parole board, and something hit me. All I could think of was, "God, I'm tired. I don't want this life for me." But it was different than I would have said it before. Because of Myriam's letters, God felt like a person, which wasn't normal. I decided to go talk to the pastor. I didn't know what to say, or how to say it, but I just told him, "I'm coming to pray and if I make the board, I'll come back and say thank you to Jesus." The pastor smiled and said, "That means you're going to come here every week?" I didn't have to think about my response, "No. I've never gone to church on the outside, and that's where I need to go. I need to stop going to church in jail to try to impress the parole board, and actually make it part of my life. I just came here to say thank you to the Lord in His House." And with that, I headed to the parole board.

I made the parole board in September of 1999 and got released that November. When I got their answer and found out that I was going home, I kept my word for the first time and went back to the church in the prison as I had promised. I went to say thank you in jail. I didn't know what to say but I knew I had to keep my promise, so I walked in, said "Thank you Jesus! Thank you for everything Lord," and left. Afterwards, I kept my word and started going to church outside of jail.

When I got home, I couldn't wait to talk to my new friend and Mom. Without hesitation, I started to get closer to my new friend, Myriam.

CHAPTER 26

PAPERS JUST IN TIME

I came home close in November 1999. I went directly to see Mom. I was given an emergency welfare check and some coupons, but I didn't want them. I was told I would be given them until I got a job, so the next morning I started searching for one. I got a job at Aramark Cafeteria Services in Citibank in midtown Manhattan. I was a utility man making $5.15 an hour.

Thank You Myriam

I really wanted to say thank you to my new best friend at the time, Myriam. The first words I spoke to her were, "Thank you for writing to me and taking care of me." I used to eat the cakes she sent me in the mornings with my coffee. I knew it was a long shot, particularly during the holidays, but I asked Myriam to go on a few dates. She agreed, and we went Christmas shopping for her daughter, and Myriam's birthday was also later in November. December was going to be a busy month for her, I could tell she was a little stressed. But, when we were together, Myriam seemed comfortable with me.

After one of our shopping trips, Myriam went to get her daughter. Myriam's daughter was two years old. Myriam had her while I was in jail and she constantly talked about her and her life as a single mom in all her letters. I didn't know it was going to be the first time I met her, but there was an instant connection. Myriam's daughter came up to me like she had known me forever. She crawled into my lap and we talked. Myriam told me that her daughter had never gotten close to any man, so it was surprising that she had trusted me so quickly.

Myriam and I started a strong bond then and it continued. Quickly, it seemed like we were going to be together, but we both had a lot of doubts. We were scared to fully invest in a romantic relationship because we had such a strong friendship foundation. I respected her in a way I had never respected a woman before. It caused Myriam so much debate that she went to Albany to clear her head and decide if this was a good choice. Myriam knew a lot about me, because I told her everything. We spoke constantly and freely. I couldn't blame Myriam for being nervous after knowing my past. I just wanted to prove to her I could be better.

Myriam had a lot of decisions to make while she was in Albany, and decided to communicate in the best way she knew how: through words. Myriam had so many doubts that she wrote a six-page letter detailing why she should and shouldn't date me. Even while Myriam was going back and forth with her decision, she continued to talk to me. It felt like we spoke constantly, and I made it clear that I wanted to continue to pursue her. Finally, Myriam agreed to let me take her to a movie. It's hard to describe how that night felt. It was almost clear. Like I finally knew my next step. Even though we weren't official, it was like we were. The conversations were enticing and deep, but there was happiness there from just being near each other.

One of the biggest motivators in her life was God, and He came up in a lot of our conversations. Myriam had insisted we go to church, and it felt right to go with her. We tried to find one we both liked, and after a few didn't work out she suggested we go to her grandmother's church. While Myriam and I were walking to the church, I realized this was the same church my girlfriend tried to bring me to when I was around 15, La Hermosa (in Chapter 18). Whatever prevented me from going to La Hermosa back then was gone now. I told Myriam about it as we were walking there and she smiled.

We sat through the whole sermon and came out excited. We both liked it. There were a lot of people who knew me from when I was a young boy. When I first walked in, a lot of the congregation turned their heads. I could hear a few whispers, "Oh my God, he's here," in both a positive and negative viewpoint. Being there, it almost felt like I was with family.

I can't say our relationship was perfect or easy. In fact, it was far from it in the beginning. We hadn't really learned to talk, but we overcame that pretty quickly. The real problem was my temper. It was nasty, and I was too harsh to Myriam. If I wasn't seeking the Lord during that time, Myriam would have left me, and rightfully so. It might be the fact that we had a common connection in church that helped teach us to communicate. That, and love.

Some time ago I blurted out, that "If I am ever going to change my life, I would like for her to be my wife." I don't know what inspired this statement to come out of my mouth. But after four months of dating, I asked Myriam to marry me. She said, "No." So, a week later I asked Myriam to marry me again and she said, "Yes." We signed the marriage license on June 22, 2000 and officially became husband and wife. We didn't have any money, so we got married in City Hall and got our marriage papers. I guess my friend Alex from prison was right after all.

My father was my best man and her best friend was there for her. That weekend, we went to Atlantic City for our honeymoon. I'll never forget the look of her face that weekend and the amount of love I had, and still have, for her. I laugh because Myriam always said she would never get married or leave New York... but she did. Out of anger, I said I would never marry another a Black or Puerto Rican woman, and I am now blessed with a black complexed, Puerto Rican.

The Citibank Papers

It wasn't even a year from the time I got out until we were married. Money was a big problem for us. In one of their seminars, Citibank offered loans to the employees of both Aramark and Citibank. I worked in the cafeteria service for Citibank so we had an opportunity. I came home and spoke to Myriam about it because I thought it could get us on the right track. Myriam looked at me with doubt. "You just came home from jail. What you gonna ask them for?" she asked. I told her $25,000, and she was stunned. "What?! $25,000? I can't even get $1,000. You gonna get $25,000?" Myriam laughed, "I've been working all my life. Good luck, Victor." I smiled and told her we had nothing to lose and that the worst they could say was no. So, I went and applied. They gave me some papers and told me they would let me know a day after the papers were turned in. I took the papers home and had Myriam help me fill them out. I turned them in the following morning.

I went to work early the next morning. The agent I met with was a regular at the cafeteria where I worked and came in that same morning. "What's good to eat?" the agent asked. Instead of telling her, I couldn't help but ask, "Did that come through yet?" She looked at me blankly and said, "Did you check your account before asking me? Or even look at an ATM?", I knew something was up. Why would she say that if it didn't go through? "No, um, there is this food over here and that food over there and I'll be right back" I mumbled, excitedly. I ran upstairs, skipping as many steps as I could, to get to the ATM. I used my card, punched in my password, and there it was. $25,000.

Myriam was stunned and surprised. Getting that Citibank loan changed our lives. We paid Myriam's school loans and other loans that we both had. We paid anyone we were indebted to and still had a little left. I saw it as a sign. After we surrendered to God, he delivered for us. God was good, and I was finally doing the right things.

CHAPTER 27

I LEARNED THIS IN JAIL.
YOU'RE HIRED!

"I learned this in jail," seemed to be my regular response when my wife asked me about something. It seemed like I was able to fix any little thing, especially around the house. I didn't have a degree but I had experience, and that seemed to get me pretty far. Those moments when I didn't seem to know right away, my wife would always tell me, "You can do it. Don't sell yourself short." Myriam gave me the motivation to better myself for our family.

Right after I got home I bumped into a friend and tried to ignore him. Mike was someone I knew from back in the day used to work on the streets as well, so I tried to stay away from him. I didn't need that in my life anymore. And distancing myself worked, until I ran into Mike on the street. He shouted, "Hey, Vic? What's going on?" I didn't say anything right away, but Mike continued to shout my name. Finally, I replied, "What's up my brother?" Mike rushed over and smiled at me. "What are you up to?" I told him I had just gotten home, and he asked if I was working. "Yeah, I work in this cafeteria. It ain't really what I'm looking for, but I gotta do what I gotta do until I get a better job," I said, softly. It wasn't that I was ashamed of my job, I just knew I could provide in a better way. "Oh yeah?" Mike asked, intrigued, "What kind of job are you looking for?" I didn't think about my response; I was just as honest as I could be. "Working in a drug program, honestly. I just want to give back, man." Mike laughed a deep, belly laugh and reached in his pocket, pulling out his business card. "Give me a call, Vic. I'm a supervisor in a drug program," Mike said, smiling as he walked away.

I went home and told my wife right away. I couldn't hide my excitement, and Myriam was supportive. Myriam wrapped her arms around me and said, "Honey, look, if that is what you want to do, then you have to do it."

I called the number on the business card the next day that Mike provided, and the support staff seemed like they expected my call. The staff hooked me up with an interview and I went over immediately. When I got there, there was one other applicant, Jose. Jose wore a suit and I could tell he had a college education by the way he talked. I didn't even have to look at his resume. When I got there, Jose was discussing what school he attended and what he had achieved already. It seemed like he just wanted to get into the position to get experience and open his own program. I lost all hope in getting the job. I wasn't nearly as qualified or confident. I was ready to give up.

I stepped outside and called my wife to tell her I was coming home. After Myriam picked up the phone and heard my voice, she instantly asked what's wrong. I told her about Jose with the Master's degree and his drive to open his own program, and she simply said, "…and?" My breath escaped, almost sounding like a laugh, "I don't have a shot, Myriam. I'm going to leave." Calmly, Myriam told me, "Stay there. You lived it, he doesn't have what you have. You have experience. All he has is school." Myriam was so kind, but I wasn't convinced. I stayed for the interview, but it was more for Myriam than it was for me.

When I got back from the call, the room was empty. Jose, with the Master's degree, must have gone in for the interview. I sat, enjoying the silence for a moment. Suddenly, the door burst open and Jose came through. "Good luck," he hastily said, "Dr. Pryor didn't let me talk at all. He shot down every single thing I had. Ha. Good luck!" Jose was annoyed, almost if that was the first time he hadn't gotten what he planned. I shook his hand and watched as he stomped away, puffing short bursts of air as he walked.

Jose's statement changed my whole mindset on how I was going to approach the interview. I knew I would have to find a way to get the upper hand without simply letting him speak. I decided I needed to talk first. I took a deep breath, walked in, and extended my hand. "My name is Victor Muniz," I said, as confidently as possible. He introduced himself as Dr. Pryor, and I immediately responded, "Sir, before we start, I want you to know that all the certificates and diplomas I have, I got in jail. In fact, I just came from jail." Dr. Pryor looked interested and said, "I'm glad you told me." I took out the certificates I had from different programs in jail and explained them. I made sure to show that I was a peer counselor and bilingual teacher's aide. I gave as much detail about what I learned in those positions and how it could help me working for a drug program.

Dr. Pryor listened until I put away the last certificate. "Since you told me about yourself," he said, sounding more human than I expected, "let me tell you a little about myself. I'm Dr. Pryor, and few people know me as Dr. Pryor, from jail. I did 25 years and decided to work on my education while I was in there. I received **all** of my degrees while serving time." It felt as though he was telling me this as if what I told him didn't make a difference. "I have one question for you, Victor Muniz. Everybody that comes here to get a job has told me they won't relapse, and of course, they do. So, what I want to know is how are you going to convince me you aren't going to relapse?" Dr. Pryor sat back after asking this, watching me intensely, but I couldn't hold back the laughter.

"Well, sir," I tried to regulate my breathing so I could talk clearly, "I was just miles away from the terrorist attacks on September 11th, when the World Trade Center was hit twice. A drug addict that is going to relapse looks for any excuse to relapse. There isn't a better excuse than that. For many people, they thought the world was going to end. If I didn't relapse then, I don't think I'll ever relapse." Dr. Pryor stood up without saying anything and slowly extended his hand. At first, I thought he was going to point to the door, but Dr. Pryor stretched his fingers out toward me. I shook his hand and he smiled, "Go back and tell Mike to welcome you to the family. You're hired!"

CHAPTER 28

FOLLOWING GOD'S PLAN

My wife always swore she would never leave New York. It was too comfortable for her and Myriam didn't want to leave what she knew. It took my son to move her. Victor Jr. was caught in a situation in Pennsylvania. He was in Jail and coming home but needed a home plan. One day, while talking to Victor Jr. on the phone, he finally came out and said it. "Hey, Papi," his voice was lower than normal, "you know I'm going to be going home eventually, I just don't have a plan yet." He sounded defeated and alone. Of course, I talked to Myriam about it right after I got off the phone with him. She calmly said, "I guess we're moving to Pennsylvania." Myriam got on the computer, as she normally does when she is trying to figure something out.

A few days later, Myriam called me from work and said, "We need to rent a car," her voice sounded flat like it was a matter of fact. "For what?" I said, surprised. We had just paid off all our bills, but we weren't really in the position to go around spending money freely. "To look at houses," she said in the same tone as before. "To look at houses?" I laughed, "We ain't got no money for a house." I couldn't see her face but I could tell she was smiling sweetly and said: "We've been pre-approved for a loan because we've been paying our debts faithfully, so it brought our credit up." I had to have her repeat it to make sure I understood correctly. In 2002, we bought a house in Pennsylvania and moved in beginning in 2003. Within a few months, my son was able to say he came home.

Pocono Community Church

If you had told me years before that moment that I would be jumping up and down and making noise in a church, I would have laughed. But on our second try, we were led to the perfect church by a girlfriend at work who was on their worship team in Pennsylvania and I couldn't have a reason not to rejoice. I had a loving, beautiful wife, a new house, and my son was home. I had every reason to worship. I started to make friends with the community there, and my wife got to know the worship team well. One afternoon the same girlfriend from the worship team asked Myriam, "Why don't you try taking Victor to Pocono Community Church? I think he'd like to worship there." Myriam didn't ask why. Instead, we decided to visit it close to Easter in 2004.

The church didn't have a building. They met in a high school. When Myriam and I got there, we were welcomed immediately and it felt like home. The congregation was mixed. There were people of all races there. The pastor was a young white man, dressed in jeans and a polo (casual), which helped us feel comfortable too. Pastor Dave was positive and knowledgeable and spoke from his heart. He was very sincere and he explained things in a way that you could understand without sounding overly educated. You could see and hear the love he had for God.

It felt as though someone had told the pastor that I would be attending because he was speaking directly to me. He wasn't condemning me and my past life. I sat in the pew speechless. It was the first time I felt fully connected to the sermon. Every word felt as though it was spoken directly at me. I never felt so guilty, saved, and grateful at the same time. This church, this pastor, challenged me. It just felt like he was talking to me and knew my life. God was working through him. After that first sermon, I knew we would become lifelong members of that church.

It was December, and while I was happy spiritually, we started to get into debt quickly. We had to get a car, we had the house, and we had to max out some credit cards while trying to get situated in Pennsylvania.

We had been attending the church for a few months at this point. Then we attended a financial seminar at church to learn how to get our finances in order. During that experience, we learned about tithing and trusting God with our money. Myriam finally looked at me and said, "Victor, we have to start tithing." Our pastors regularly discussed how credit, finances, and tithing, or donating to the church. Myriam usually handled the money and paid all the bills. At the beginning of the month, she would always say, "Don't touch the money." This was extremely important at the beginning of the year since we usually had larger bills to pay such as the house insurance. Myriam would then pay all the bills we needed, and if we had any left, we were lucky. Usually, we had to use credit cards to make ends meet, but we paid the minimum balance so we could stay afloat. "Are you sure we need to tithe? We don't have extra money," I asked. "We say we trust God, we have faith in God and we love God, but we're not really trusting him," she replied. "Okay, if you say so, but we can't even pay our bills. I don't know how we can tithe."

I trusted her, and she trusted God. January came quickly, and I was worried that she would tell me we had run out of money since the first of the year was always the most expensive. I remember nervously sitting in the same room, waiting for her to say something. But she never did. Myriam didn't even ask me for money or tell me not to touch it. Finally, I confronted her: "Honey, what happened? Why haven't you asked me for insurance money." Myriam simply said, "Don't ask me how, but everything is paid for." That's the way God works. When you're obedient and fully surrender to do what God asks you to do, He'll always see you through any situation.

CHAPTER 29

STRUGGLES NEVER END

I never talked about it a lot, but when we were in New York I was baptized. It was on November, 26, 2000, my wife Myriam's birthday. When I came home from jail the last time and started seeing Myriam we decided to go to church. We had tried a few churches and finally settled on one. This happens to be the exact same church that I was invited to earlier in my youth by one of my first love, Maria. Once Myriam and I started attending church regularly, getting baptized felt like the right next step.

There are some things that stick with you throughout your life and being baptized is certainly one of them, especially for me. On the day we were baptized, Paquita, one of the elders at church, who had grown very close to us, said to me, "Don't think things are going to become good or better because you became a Christian. That's not how it works. Things are going to be rough in your life." And she was right, there were rough points. In fact, right after we got baptized is when I bumped into Joe, coming up out of the train station. This incident immediately brought what the elder at church had told me to mind. Despite this setback, overall things were pretty good. I had a strong son and a loving wife. I was happy in Pennsylvania. We finally got out of over $100,000 in debt while tithing the entire time. It all seemed like we could finally start new, and I thanked God for that.

Cancer

Things were looking up for the most part, at least, they were until 2011. Every year I got the flu shot and was complaining about a sore throat for a couple days prior to my appointment. Eventually, I had complained about it so much that my wife said, "You need to go tell the doctor." I laughed it off, telling her it was just a cold. Within the next few weeks, I had my annual check-up and flu shot. After looking me over, my doctor asked if I was ready for my flu shot. I admitted I had a cold and a sore throat, and the doctor instantly told me to get back on the table. "Why didn't you tell me you weren't feeling well," she asked as she grabbed the tongue depressor. The doctor asked me to open my mouth, and I could see the concerned look on her eyes as she peered in my mouth. "Your throat looks angry," was all she said, and she walked to the phone on the wall. The doctor picked it up and made a phone call, but she was so quiet I couldn't hear what she was saying. After she hung up, the doctor looked at me and told me I needed to see an oral surgeon. With a serious face, she said, "I've called someone I know and he can see you immediately. I don't feel comfortable with you waiting until tomorrow." So, I went; I didn't have an option.

    I got the oral surgeon's address from the receptionist and headed that way. I was worried since my doctor insisted on me meeting with an oral surgeon immediately. But I walked in, told the receptionist I was there to see the oral surgeon, and was sent right back. The doctor looked quickly at my throat, told me he didn't like the way it looked, and asked me to make another appointment in a month. I set an appointment on the way out and called my doctor to tell her the news. "No," my doctor said with a sense of anger in her voice, "It can't be. I need you to go sooner than a month. Call him every day to see if someone has cancelled." I couldn't believe she was asking me to constantly bother him. "I don't want to call every day and make him angry." My doctor let out a long, loud sigh, "He won't even know you made the calls. In fact, he won't know about the calls at all. You will be talking to the receptionist and setting it up. Everyone does it. Just call **every, single, day.**" She emphasized the last three words before hanging up.

I did exactly as the doctor told me to. Every day, I would call the oral surgeon's office and ask if there were any cancellations, and day after day the receptionist would tell me there were none. At the end of every call I would tell the receptionist, "Have a blessed day". And after 8 days, she finally said there was a cancellation and she could get me in tomorrow. "Absolutely. I'll be there. Thank you," I said, unsure if there was an actual cancelation or if the receptionist was just annoyed with me calling.

I got to the surgeon's office and went through the same process as I had a little over a week ago, and again I was sent back immediately. The surgeon looked thoroughly at my throat, spending much longer than last time. He stepped out of the room without saying a word, and came back with a large syringe attached to a huge needle. Following behind him was a nurse, who looked nervously at me. The doctor asked me to open my mouth again without telling me much else. I did as he asked, feeling tense. I just knew he was going to put the injection in my throat. A few seconds went by in silence. He continued looking around, moving the needle at different angles but not injecting anything yet. I wanted to beg him to do it. Just to get it over with. But I remained silent. Finally, after around a minute, he blurted "I'm not touching it. It looks too bad." The doctor handed the needle to his nurse and pulled his rubber gloves off. He left the room quickly. His nurse, looking slightly confused while holding the needle, followed.

I sat, staring at the clock. I had no idea what was going on, but after seeing that needle I knew it was something bad. Another minute ticked by without anyone coming in. All of the posters on the walls were outdated. The floor was cold, but I tried to look for images in the patterns to distract myself. Three more minutes. The room started feeling smaller. My eyes kept going back to the cotton swabs, alcohol, and tongue depressors near the sink and the red, hazard box where they placed all the used needles. The needle that was meant for me wasn't in it. My throat looked so bad that a trained doctor was too scared to give me a shot.

Another four minutes, thirty-eight seconds. The clock continued ticking relentlessly. Finally, the door squeaked open.

The nurse appeared, trying to put on a smile. "Victor, we called your doctor. I made an appointment with a throat specialist. You have an appointment later today." I wanted to ask what all of that was, why he was so concerned, what the doctor meant. I wanted to know what was wrong. I opened my mouth to ask, but I heard my voice, somewhat foreign, simply say "Okay."

I got the address and went to the specialist that afternoon. The waiting room was full, which was a relief. At least, it was until the receptionist sent me right back to see the specialist. He took one look at my throat and said, "I am pretty sure it's cancer, but that's not official. I have to take a biopsy to verify that. What are you doing Monday?" It was Friday when I saw him, so I assumed this was as quickly as he could get me in. My mind went on autopilot. "On Monday? I'm doing whatever you tell me to do," my voice sounded robotic. Even now, years later, I can't describe what was going on in my mind. Life became a blur.

They scheduled the biopsy for 7:00 am Monday morning. I can barely remember what happened between that appointment and when the results came back. I know Myriam was there, and positive as always, but my mind went blank. It was the specialist's phone call that broke me out of the haze. "Victor?" He asked. I don't know if I responded, but I think I did. "It's positive. You have cancer, and we need to act quickly. We will start to get a team together to work on it." Somewhere in me, I didn't expect this. It's like I knew the worst was a possibility, but I didn't think that I would go through that. I had gone through so much already, and I had God on my side. Yet, here I was. A cancer patient. "Thanks, doctor." The words formed without me knowing. I'm not sure I was actually thankful in that moment, but I was at a loss for anything else to say. I didn't know what else to say, so I hung up the phone.

At church the following Sunday, I went next to the stage to meet with the pastor, Dave, right after the sermon. I told him about my circumstances. Well, I was more direct. "I have throat cancer," I blurted. I didn't know how else to introduce the topic. He asked how I felt, and my only response was that I gave it to God. He placed his hands gently on my throat and prayed for me and my family.

Meanwhile, I started attending church more and more. I needed to feel some kind of normalcy. The first Wednesday of every month was prayer night, and while I hated talking about my condition I thought having people pray for me would be good. Pastor Dave was there, and he told the group about my condition so I wouldn't have to. I wasn't embarrassed, until he asked me to come to the front stage. A group of men circled around me, leaving me no room to escape. They each laid their hands on my shoulders or head and prayed aloud for my family and recovery. It was the first-time strangers touched me in a kind, caring way. It was more intimate than a handshake or hug; I felt like I was part of their family.

I had three doctors working intensely on my case. I can't remember a time in my life where I talked about how I was feeling or my "situation" more. Most of my days felt like they were spent talking to Dr. Raymond, Dr. Hyzinski, or Dr. Frattali. More and more of my days were spent on the phone or traveling to treatment. Dr. Hyzinski was my chemotherapy doctor, and he tried to make me the most comfortable through the process. There were a lot of medicines I had to pick up at the pharmacy before I started chemo, which made me even more uncomfortable. I wasn't used to taking medicine, so this became a whole new world. When I walked in, his first words to me were "These ladies here," he said, pointing at his nurses, "are going to take care of you." I was a little overwhelmed to trust my situation in another set of hands. But the nurses sat my wife and I down and discussed the process in detail. They told me what to expect, how I would feel, and how to best take care of the side effects. "After God, you are in the best hands possible," One of the nurses said, smiling as she left the room. I felt a sense of relief, and almost thought that I could be strong enough to battle the cancer.

I started taking chemo regularly, and Dr. Ramon was the one who gave me radiation. I would get both at the same time. They told me from the start that it was something that they don't usually do. Normally, patients would get one then the other, but they said that "we needed to act aggressively to counteract how it is growing. If we don't act, we would have to operate and remove a piece of your tongue and you may never speak again or have to learn to speak again." It was the first time I was simply in the hands of another person. Whatever they asked, I did. Myriam and I agreed, we needed to do all we could and trust in God.

I went from 184 to 116 pounds. My throat was too inflamed and tender from the treatment to eat, so I didn't. Water temperature impacted my ability to drink, so if it was not room temperature I couldn't stomach it. The lack of water hurt my kidneys, and they went down to 13% effectiveness. Quickly, I was switched to dialysis by the kidney doctor. Within hours, Dr. Hyzinski came in after chemo to talk about the change in my condition. I became dehydrated and asked my wife to take me to the emergency room from where I was hospitalized. A kidney doctor (Nephrologist) came to see me and told me my kidneys were functioning at 13% and if they didn't improve I would need dialysis. Dr. Hyzinski walked in and said I would not need dialysis because my kidney function would improve by Thursday, which was two days later.

Myriam and I were trying to stay positive, but I started to feel defeated. "You're looking good," the doctor said, smiling as he walked in. I couldn't help but laugh. There is no way I could have looked good. "Doctor," I breathless laughed, "How could I look good? I lost all this weight and now my kidneys are failing? I've got needles here and here and here," I said, pointing all over my body. "You're alive and talking," he said, smiling. "You look real good, Victor." But I had started to doubt. It seemed like I couldn't get above it.

The next morning, my phone rang. "I hope you're feeling good," a voice told me. I didn't recognize it at first, so I didn't respond. "Feel better, Victor. Let me pray for you." After that, I knew it was one of my brothers from church. I didn't have the energy to say anything, so I just listened. While he was praying, Dr. Hyzinski walked in and waited for me to notice him. After a few minutes, the guy from church finished praying over me and wished me luck before he hung up. Dr. Hyzinski stood in the corner, waiting. I apologized and explained the situation, and he simply responded with, "We all need prayers."

I had a lot of small issues and situations in the hospital, but I always prayed. One of the biggest was when they told me they were going to have to test my bladder because the cancer might had moved down. The medical team didn't tell me what the test was for exactly. My kidneys were bad, so they were scared something might be wrong there as well. They were in a rush to figure out what was going on. Normally, when they do checks on a bladder they have the patient empty it before so they can get better images of what is going on. I was never told to empty my bladder, so when they took the tests it was full. Once they noticed this, they put a catheter in. The medical team didn't need to, but since I was under anesthesia, it wasn't the easiest at the time but unnecessary. Myriam was furious, and I threatened to take it off herself if they didn't fix it, which eventually caused them to do what was right.

Throughout everything, my motto was that "everything was alright". I would repeat it to anyone, even if I knew that wasn't the case. When he came to visit, I told Pastor Dave this, but he didn't believe me. Pastor Dave brought his wife to come visit me, but throughout their visit I told them that everything was okay and I was leaving it in God's hands, even if I wasn't fully sure I was capable of doing so. "I came here to minister to you, and you're preaching to me," Pastor Dave laughed. "Let's just pray. Is that okay?" We prayed for me, my doctors, my nurses, for everything.

Few things changed. Four days later, I was still in the hospital, but

Myriam tried to keep my spirits up. They decided to give me a feeding tube since I couldn't eat. The kidney specialist and Dr. Hyzinski were debating about kidney dialysis. Dr. Hyzinski was fully convinced I wasn't going on dialysis. "Trust me," he said, "By Thursday, you will be getting better." It was Tuesday, and it seemed impossible to see any improvement. I felt weaker and more exhausted than I had felt in my whole life, but it was nice to hear that someone thought I would get better. I could tell by the kidney specialist's response that he highly doubted Dr. Hyzinski's beliefs.

Wednesday was difficult, but I kept hearing Dr. Hyzinski's voice in my head. I just had to get to Thursday. Even though I was physically and emotionally drained, I had one more round of radiation. Since they thought I was going to be on dialysis, the doctors and staff at the hospital were refusing to let me leave. Once again, Dr. Hyzinski stood up for me: "He is leaving. His wife will take him to get his last radiation treatment, because if he doesn't take that one, all of the others would have been for nothing. Every one of those previous 32 sessions would be useless. He will go." And that's exactly what happened. My wife took me to the last treatment and brought me back.

First thing Thursday morning, Dr. Hyzinski walked into my room with a huge smile on your face. "Your kidneys are showing signs of improvement, Victor," he said with confidence. "It looks like you're starting to get better." At that moment, I realized the impact God had on my life. There were so many times I could have, and should have, died. Every time I thought it was finally over, God proved to me it wasn't. But each time, I found myself okay, and the only reason I could find was my surrender to God's will and his protection. Today, my kidneys are 100% and I'm cancer free.

CHAPTER 30

ENTERING THE MINISTRY

While in New York, my wife and I were finding God. One of my wife's friends, Sonia, came up and said, "I need you to do something for me." I was a newcomer to the church scene and wanted to make sure their friendship continued, so I told her I would do it if I could. Sonia told me that her church had a prison ministry and they held a service in jail each week. "Could you come with me and my church to Rikers Island and give a testimony?" she asked, innocently. Because Sonia knew my background, she thought it would be a good fit. I agreed and told her that it wouldn't be a problem, but I had never done anything like that before. I never thought of doing it.

When we got to Rikers, I was greeted by a C.O. at the door. I couldn't have expected what was going to happen next, even if I tried. "Victor? Victor Muniz?", the C.O. asked. "Yes, sir," I said hesitantly. "I never thought I would see you walking through these doors," he laughed, opening the door wider for me. I didn't even remember this particular C.O., but he seemed to remember me that he called me by name. The C.O. looked familiar, but I honestly don't know if he was my C.O. at the time or how he knew me. Maybe he had heard of me before. Either way, it was a kindness I was not used to from C.O.'s. I went in to start setting up.

Sonia from church was already there when I arrived. We were in a decent sized auditorium with chairs all facing in one direction. Sonia was facing the empty chairs and smiled when she saw me. "We're going to worship and then I'll announce you and let them know you are going to give a testimony," she said. Sonia's voice was calm as if she had done this several times before. I felt my heart start to race a little, and I couldn't help but think about being an inmate in one of those chairs.

The inmates started filling into the seats. What happened before my introduction was a blur; I'm not sure if I was just focused on what I would say or if the whole situation was out of character, but I was taken back to reality when I heard Sonia say, "Victor Muniz!" I stood up and started walking to the front of the room. I hadn't prepared a speech or really even practiced. I assumed since I had been on the other side of the room, everything would come naturally.

I vaguely remember introducing myself to the inmates, but what I do recall is the look in their eyes. Most had already glossed over, like there was nothing to actually listen to. They seemed almost bored. "I was in jail so often, I used to leave my spoon, fork, and toothbrush because I knew I would be back within a few months, at the most," I said, hoping to spark some connection. A few guys looked up, but most weren't connected. I started walking while I talked, and overheard a guy in the third row: "I'm tired of these Christians coming here that never actually been in jail saying they have. They don't know nothing about how we feel in here. They don't know what it's like to be incarcerated."

He clearly wasn't trying to whisper and you could see the anger on his face. I heard myself pause, and tried to recollect myself as quickly as possible. The guy behind him fidgeted for a few moments and finally tapped him on the shoulder. He leaned forward, "That's Victor from 115th man!" The anger left his face, followed by disbelief. "The Victor?! From 115th and Lexington?!" he asked, turning around in his chair. The second guy nodded. I didn't know either of them, but they had heard of me. Because of my prison experiences, my reputation preceded me. Apparently, that was enough. The guy from the third row met my eyes and sat quietly, now actively listening.

Before I realized it, I came to a closing. I wasn't sure how to end it. I hadn't really prepared anything. "I'm going to close with a prayer," my voice said. It didn't even sound like me. "I'm going to pray for you.

I'm also going to do something I never thought I would do in my entire life: I'm going to pray for the C.O.s as well. We all need Prayer."

The prison meeting sparked a passion in me that I had never thought would be there. I took pride in speaking to inmates and trying to get them to listen. Even if they didn't, knowing that I could pray for them and with them, made me feel as though I could help others in some way. When we moved to Pennsylvania and started going to Pocono Community Church, I introduced myself to the Pastor, Dave, and gave him a rundown of my life. A few months later, after his service, Pastor Dave stopped me in the hallway. He told me that he had a job for me: "I need you to go down to the prison and visit this young man named Greg. His family is part of this church." Instantly, I thought of the Pastor Andrew who visited my father while I was in jail and asked to help pay my bond. (in Chapter 19, The Drug Game) Pastor Andrew was so kind to me and made me feel welcome. So, I went to meet with Pastor Dave the following day to talk about the young man, Greg, he wanted me to visit in prison.

When I got to the jail, I checked in. Greg's family was there, so I only spoke to him for about 15 minutes because I didn't want to take too much of his family's time. There is a limited block of time for visitation once a week and I wanted to be sure that his family had enough time to spend with him. When I spoke to Greg, he broke down and maintained his innocence. When I got back to my car, it hit me. I felt like I couldn't even really remember what I said, but I saw that it broke him down and it broke me down when I got to the car. I sat in the car and called my wife. I told her, "This is the first time I felt the presence of God. I don't remember what I said. It's like it wasn't me speaking. It was God." After that experience, I was sold. This was the life for me. After that moment, Pastor Dave called me anytime he knew someone was in trouble. And when Pastor Dave called, I would go wherever he asked and talked.

As Pocono Community Church grew, I grew in helping inmates. Eventually, the Pocono Community Church moved into their own a new building and I took the position of Prison Ministry Director. I found a new kind of passion for helping others get out of the same situation I was in. To do my job better, I started reaching out to the community. I got involved with a married couple, Dr. Alma and Dr. Carlos Colon with the Born Again Ministry and they inspired me to get into jails to teach. However, each jail I applied to denied me.

Finally, Dr. Alma called. Right when I picked up the phone, she yelled, "I can't believe it!" before I could even say hello. I laughed and said, "Why don't you tell me what it is so I can see if I can believe it or not." I could hear her smile over the phone, "You've been accepted to go into the jail to teach!" I haven't turned back since. I volunteer to do so because I feel connected to God through those in need. I just hope I can inspire others to do the same.

EPILOGUE:
REAL TALK WITH VICTOR

For God so loved the world, that he gave his only begotten Son, that whosoever believeth in him shall not perish, but have everlasting life.
-John 3:16

I have changed my legacy from 1240 to 3:16, by realizing that God was always with me, loving me and forgiving me. We have to forgive as God forgave us in John 3:16, so that we can change our legacies. It took me my whole life to learn how to forgive but, without me knowing it, God was always with me guiding me and he's there guiding you as well. Earlier in my life my father's girlfriend, Mom, was a great example of God's love. Mom always encouraged me, cared for me and believing in me, even when I was at my worst. Even though I still look back at my past and get upset at times, forgiveness has allowed me to move on. This isn't the kind of forgiveness that I had on the street. On the streets, forgiveness meant letting it settle but never forgetting. I wasn't even the type to forgive that way. If you did me dirty, I got angry and I got even. I had to learn to truly forgive. It is, by far, one of the hardest things I have ever learned to do.

When you don't forgive, you actually hurt yourself more. Forgiveness allows you to release the anger you are holding and let you move on. While you are making yourself sick with anger, the other person isn't even thinking about what happened. It took me a long time to realize that other people move on and forget what happened while you still hold on. Finding God helped me learn that, which gave me so much freedom.

Forgiving my grandmother (Mama) was my first step. I honestly felt like she had poured all her love into my brother, leaving me as a second thought and ignored. I didn't have the wisdom to understand why my grandmother treated me the way she did. Now that I'm older and accepted God in my life, I realized how much she loved me. I wish I could go back and apologize and let her know I forgive her. I was a different person than my brother, and we needed different types of love. Mama knew she had to be stronger and stricter because I grew up rapidly and reminded her of her own son, my father. Because Mama had raised my father, she already knew the path I was headed. Mama wanted the best for me, and that was her way of showing it.

"Honor your father and your mother, so that you may live long in the land the Lord your God is giving you." -Exodus 20:12

Earlier in my life I had to get over the deep desire to get even with my father. I had a lot of hate for my father, and it caused me to want to get even. I craved revenge that wasn't for me, and it took finding God to realize that. It was never necessarily about him, but more about his actions. What he did to my mother (Mami) destroyed me, but I knew I was supposed to love him. When I finally rose up and avenged my mother, by punching him in the face, it felt empty and caused more damage. Punching him left me truly torn and hurt.

Even before I found God, I realize now that it was with God's help that I was able to build the relationship I always wanted with my father. It allowed our relationship to become stronger. We became best friends, and I even asked him to be the best man at my wedding. But when I forgave him, I forgave him 100%. Forgiving my father freed him as well. I remember watching a movie with my father right before he died and there was a scene where the main actor hit his wife. My father got irritated and upset, and I could see that he saw himself in the main character. The last 14 years I got to spend with my father before he passed were by far the best because we both forgave, which allowed us to change for the better.

"Do not take revenge, my dear friends, but leave room for God's wrath, for it is written: 'It is mine to avenge; I will repay,' says the Lord".
-Romans 12:19

The lifestyle I lived meant there were a lot of people to forgive, and the next was the man who tried to kill me with the shotgun, Joe. Joe was Nate's cousin from the Ceelo game all those years ago. After I was baptized, I headed back home for a while. Even after I accepted God, when I went back to 116th and Lexington I had to stay aware. I remember regularly sticking my hand in my pocket so it would look like I was reaching for a weapon.

My wife and I lived in a 4th-floor walkup on 115th between 2nd and 3rd Avenue. I was walking up the stairs from the subway station on 116th and Lexington Avenue coming home from work. It had been so many years I didn't think I would bump into Joe, but I knew it could happen. As I was walking up the stairs one evening, raised my head, I found myself staring right into Joe's eyes. My mind flashed back and I remembered scrambling across the street, trying to dodge the bullets of his shotgun. When Joe realized it was me, his face turned pale.

We were stuck since Joe was trying to head down the stairwell. I had been thinking about this situation for a while, so I did what I thought was right. I simply hugged him and told him God loved him. I didn't know what else to say. Joe looked back, shocked, and said: "Victor, if you need anything, ask me for it." I have no idea what made him respond so calmly. Maybe it was that I wasn't confrontational. Maybe he had found God too. Maybe he was ready to forgive as well. All I know was that it became a teaching point for me. There was a fear that I didn't realize before that disappeared. It moved me so much that I shared it with my pastor, and he asked me to share it with the congregation.

> *"Jesus looked at them and said, 'With man this is impossible, but*
> *with God all things are possible.'" -Matthew 19:26*

Forgiving the man who killed my brother is still a challenge. I wanted my revenge so bad that I would plead guilty even if I wasn't near the scene. I thought I would be able to get closer to him but it never happened. I held that hatred in my heart for 43 years and thought about it almost daily, but I was going to church and felt I had a handle on it. It wasn't until December 2016, while Pastor Dave was preaching on forgiveness, that I realized the impact my brother's death was causing me. During that service, I wept while sitting in my seat. I've done lots of difficult things in my life, but few of them were harder than forgiving the man that killed my own blood. Knowing that God had the strength to forgive the people who crucified him, gave me motivation.

Every two years, I get a letter from the state asking me to participate in the parole board when this man comes before the parole commission. I used to instantly rip it up. I knew I couldn't see or even write about that. I didn't want to take the time because I was afraid of my own reaction and how it would impact me. It happened faithfully: every two years I would get the letter, and every two years I would rip it up. I got the last letter in January 2019, and I planned to travel to the parole board and meet that man in person. I didn't know the procedure. I didn't know if I would be allowed to speak or if I would just get the chance to listen, but I knew what I would say if I got the chance to say something.

I did not get to travel to the parole board hearing in January, but I spoke with the parole commissioner on the phone. They asked me how my brother's death had affected my life. Describing how I felt about my brother's killer and the impact it had on my life was one of the hardest things I've ever had to do, but this is what I said, "I'm not telling you one way or the other, to let him go or not. I trust that you know what's best. But I want you to know that I forgive him." Although I forgave the man that killed my brother, I believe that I was really forgiving myself.

"God cannot forgive those that don't forgive others. You can't expect to get what you don't give. So, take it all to God in prayer and he will free you." -Victor Muniz

We all ask God for forgiveness. It's the hardest thing to do because of pride. And God forgives those who forgive others. You can't expect to get what you don't give. The bible says, "14 For if you forgive other people when they sin against you, your heavenly Father will also forgive you. 15 But if you do not forgive others their sins, your Father will not forgive your sins. (Matthew 6:14-15). So, when you say that you forgive someone for what they have done to you, did you forgive or did you really forgive?

I've talked to guys in jail that say the right things about forgiveness but don't really mean it. They still have revenge in their hearts. The forgiveness was not genuine. Hate and wanting revenge is a prison too.

I had to learn that revenge was never mine to take. It was always the Lord's. So I say, take it all to God in prayer and he will free you.

Writing this book has helped me put the pieces together and has become therapeutic. While it is just a taste of my life, I hope it resonates with you. We all know someone going through at least one of the situations in these chapters, or we have personally gone through something similar.

My goal with this book was to connect to those moments and remind people not to judge but rather to help and forgive. I know I cannot save the world, but my hope is to encourage at least one person to understand forgiveness then he/she could change someone else's life and so on and so on. If I can reach just one person, then I know that I'm doing what God has intended.

Have a Blessed Day.

44366265R00090

Made in the USA
Middletown, DE
10 May 2019